STRIKE
DEFENSE
MANUAL

STRIKE
DEFENSE
MANUAL

Walter G. Mullins

Gulf Publishing Company
Book Division
Houston, London, Paris, Tokyo

Strike Defense Manual

Library of Congress Cataloging in Publication Data

Mullins, Walter G   1939-
    Strike defense manual.

    Includes index.
    1.   Strikes and lockouts—United States.   I.   Title.
HD5324.M87   658.3′154   80-14961
ISBN 0-87201-812-1

Contents

Acknowledgments

In a variety of ways many people have contributed, if not directly to the work itself, then to the person who wrote it.

To the extent the manual achieves its goal, I credit my mother and father for the example they set. I am also grateful to have worked with such skilled tacticians and negotiators as Garland Bearden and Richard Blum. I extend special thanks to Lee Smith for his review of the original manuscript.

Were it not for the patience and understanding of my wife Shirley, the manual would not have been completed. Finally, a note of special recognition is due my six-year-old, Nick, without whom it might have been finished somewhat sooner.

Preface

In management circles the spectre of a strike has often been viewed synonymously with fire, flood, and famine. Companies large and small have anticipated impending walk-outs with visions of plant shutdowns, customer defections, employee ill will, even financial ruin.

Historically, the strike has often lived up to its reputation. As a result, rather than take one on, management often yields to union demands it would much rather deny.

Further, there is little to indicate that the incidence of strikes is on the wane. Regardless how the statistics are interpreted, the fact remains that thousands of strikes occur in this country each year. Thousands more are avoided only through distasteful compromise by management on important issues. The losses suffered by employers in both instances are incalculable.

While much has been written about the current state of affairs, management can derive little encouragement from it. Strikes are described, analyzed, categorized, predicted, even occasionally criticized, but the thrust of the literature remains that a priori they cause losses to employers. One might properly conclude that the strike is a disease for which there is no treatment.

The colossal irony of this situation is that it need not exist at all. The plain truth is the strike is only as menacing, only as devastating, only as "incurable" as employers believe it to be. The power of the strike lies simply in the fact that it is feared, and therein lies the reason for this manual. In the simplest terms its purpose is to enable any employer to deal firmly and fairly with unions, confident that if forced to take a strike, the company can win it. It is management's "prescription" for victory. Taken as directed the information in this manual will show the reader how to win strikes.

By definition the function of any manual is to provide practical instructions that enable the reader to attain a specific goal. Put another way, the purpose of this manual is to make you a winner.

Walt Mullins
April 1980

Introduction

The withholding of services by employees, striking, has played a large role in the American labor drama for almost two hundred years.

To those who consider the power and influence of American unions a curse on the land, it will come as no surprise that they were born of an English plague.

In 1348 the Black Death swept feudal England, eliminating half the labor force. Employers in the developing towns and cities faced a severe shortage of workers. The serfs responded, leaving the manors to demand the higher wages the scarcity of workers would force the merchants to pay. Laws were enacted in 1349 and 1350 to stem both the migration to the cities and the spiraling, sometimes concerted, wage demands. In 1548, Parliament felt compelled to condemn as a criminal conspiracy any combination of workmen that sought higher wages or shorter hours. In 1611, English courts struck down worker combinations per se, regardless of provable intent. But the die had been cast.

By 1720, the first recognizable English labor unions were formed. They were composed of the skilled craftsmen of that era, such as shoemakers and tailors. In 1721, a group of the latter was indicted and found guilty of conspiring among themselves to raise their wages. Another century passed before the status of English unions was formally legalized by acts of Parliament in 1824 and 1825. Most strikes by unions remained criminal acts until 1875, and actions against union activities as civil conspiracies continued to receive judicial support until 1906.

The American experience was similar, with the first union (Philadelphia Cordwainers) organized in 1794 and its leaders found guilty of criminal conspiracy in 1806.

However, unions continued to multiply and utilize the strike in their efforts to persuade employers. In 1842, a Massachusetts court gave

1

labor an important judicial recognition, holding, on the facts of the particular case, that neither the union nor its methods were per se illegal.

This decision did not, however, result in a national acceptance of the labor movement, and successful actions against the legality of unions and the actions of their leaders continued into this century. Yet, the growth of labor throughout this and later periods was impressive. In the 1850's, permanent national craft unions were formed. The Noble Order of the Knights of Labor was formed in 1869, its purpose being to unite all workers, skilled and unskilled, into a national political and economic organization. Its membership numbered over 700,000 before an organization of national craft unions formed in 1880 supplanted it. This latter group became the American Federation of Labor and, ultimately, after it merged with an organization composed of unions it had previously expelled, the AFL-CIO. (Today this organization numbers in its membership 13½ of the nation's 20 million organized workers.)

The early American labor organizations were often highly visionary, certainly in large part because they lacked the strength to engage the nation's industries in direct combat. They espoused such causes as free education for all, universal suffrage, and restrictions on child labor. Overall, until the 1930's, labor did not capture America's essentially agrarian, laissez faire heart. The Great Depression, however, brought about a dramatic shift in public opinion. With the nation's industries at a standstill and unemployment a national plague, Congress responded.

Federal legislation enacted during this period, most notably the National Labor Relations Act of 1935, was intended to and did encourage unions to organize America's workers. The pendulum swung and labor found itself, with federal backing and its successful organizing drives of the 30's and 40's behind it armed to the teeth.

It seems that is still the case today, and, among the many weapons at the disposal of organized labor, the strike is acknowledged to be the most powerful. Undoubtedly, it is this potency of the strike that explains the continuing efforts to develop an alternative to it.

Compulsory arbitration and fact finding have been advanced as reasonable methods for avoiding strikes. Some states, in fact, have included them in the statutes governing the bargaining relationship between state agencies and public employees. Some private collective bargaining agreements also specify that some or all issues the parties are unable to resolve through negotiations will be referred to an impartial decision-maker.

Other students of the subject recommend improvements in communications between the parties, through greater, perhaps even mandatory, involvement of the Federal Mediation and Conciliation Service. Still others recommend industry- and/or nationwide bargaining.

Perhaps an acceptable alternative will be found. It has yet to happen, and, for most employers, the union's assault gun remains primed and ready.

Your company may have had a long and generally harmonious relationship with its union(s). There may even exist a conscious or not-so-conscious feeling that the union is such a friend of management that it could never bring itself to strike. Do not deceive yourself. If the time comes when the company takes a firm stand that the union for political, policy, or economic reasons cannot accept, that union will strike and strike hard. And it will bring into play every resource at its command. No union calls a strike it has even the faintest intention of losing.

By definition and in practice strikes are not friendly. Make no mistake about it, if your employees go on strike they will do so for one reason: To shut you down and force you to your knees. There are no "friends of management" on the picket line.

There is but one response to a strike that makes sense, and that is to win it. Hands down.

There are two elements to winning: (a) continuing your operation, and (b) avoiding any illegal action prior to or during the strike that will enable the union to prevail anyway.

Winning is not simple. Continuing your operations requires concentrated advance preparation and superb communications. Avoiding illegal action demands the consistent application of informed judgment. It is hard work, but it is worth it. And there is really no acceptable substitute for it.

This manual has been prepared so that if you have the will to win, you also have the way. Here are the requisites for success.

Being Prepared. This means taking steps now, before the strike, which will enable you to keep operating during the strike. There is much to be done, and this manual will show you step-by-step how to prepare your game plan. Many of the procedural preparations, such as the formation of strike committees, the training of new hires, etc., are applicable to virtually all companies. Some, because no two organizations are exactly alike, will require simple adaptation to your operation.

Communicating. All the people involved in your strike response must be kept abreast of what is happening. Proper communication takes time but there is no success without it. This manual provides a detailed blueprint for ensuring that each player knows the game plan and his or her assignment. (Throughout the remainder of the book the male pronoun will be used. This is merely for convenience. The substantial and ever-increasing role of females in labor and management is well recognized.)

Avoiding Illegal Strike-Related Actions. One wrong move can render meaningless a superbly conceived strike response. This manual will point out many pitfalls to avoid and help you develop the ability to spot situations in which judgment must precede action.

A caveat: Labor law is exceedingly complex and constantly evolving. A seemingly minor fact variation can and does produce dissimilar National Labor Relations Board and court rulings in apparently comparable situations. It is difficult to generalize what you can and cannot legally do in strike situations. There is, however, an underlying, two-fold premise of the law that you should learn now and carefully review before you take any strike-related action. It is that (a) you cannot interfere with the right of employees to engage in concerted activity for their mutual aid and protection (which includes the right to strike), and (b) you cannot discriminate between strikers and non-strikers. A simple example of the former is discharging an employee because he goes out on a legal strike, and of the latter, offering to pay replacements more than was offered the strikers.

Unfortunately, most strike questions are not simple and require careful analysis prior to action. Obviously, you want to win the strike in your plant *and* in court, so do not take unnecessary chances. Obtain the counsel of a competent labor attorney. It will pay you handsomely.

To further assist you, there are forms, checklists, and sample memoranda, which are referred to as "exhibits," in the back of this manual that are to be used in your strike preparations. You are going to be dealing with a great volume of data from all areas of your operation, and it must be accurately assimilated and coordinated. Further, a large number of people will be given important information-gathering assignments, and they must be given the format by which to prepare it fully (so they will not have to go back again and again) and consistently (so all the data from all sources will mesh into a usable source of action). Note also that these forms are not to be completed just once. They will be one of the cornerstones of your strike response, and you will refer to them often. Therefore, they must be kept current; many should be updated each week. The forms included in the back of this manual are only suggested designs. You will no doubt redo them to fit your particular needs and your operation. The important thing is to use them.

A Strike By
Any Other Name . . .

The law that will govern most aspects of your activities during a strike is the National Labor Relations Act, as amended by the Labor-Management Relations Act of 1947, and the Labor-Management Reporting and Disclosure Act of 1959. As used in this manual, the terms "NLRA" and the "Act" refer to the act in its amended form. The NLRA grants employees the right to organize and requires employers to bargain with the employee representative (normally a union) regarding wages, hours, and working conditions. This law also defines both employer and union unfair labor practices. The federal agency that administers the Act is the National Labor Relations Board.

Bear this in mind: The NLRA was conceived and written to promote the unionization of employees. The Act itself states in part: "Experience has proved that protection by law of the right of employees to organize and bargain collectively safeguards commerce from injury, impairment, or interruption..." Therefore, anticipate now that the burden will be on you to prove that your actions did not interfere with "protected" employee rights. It may not always be easy, but if you looked before you leaped, you can do it.

There are several types of strikes recognized under federal labor law, and you should be aware of them.

Economic Strike

In essence this is a strike to force an employer to grant the union's economic demands. It commonly occurs when a union is unable to achieve its goals at the bargaining table. Economic strikers may be permanently replaced but not discharged. Upon unconditional application, an economic striker is entitled to reinstatement immediately unless he has been permanently replaced. However, even if that has occurred, he is entitled to reinstatement upon the departure of his replacement unless in the interim he has obtained other regular and substantially equivalent employment or the employer can show legitimate and substantial business reasons for not reinstating him (such as a valid elimination of his job). The Labor Board has rather pointedly refused to place a time limit on the reinstatement rights of strikers.

Unfair Labor Practice Strike

This is a strike caused or prolonged by an employer's unfair labor practice(s). Employer unfair labor practices are defined in Section 8. (a) of the NLRA and include: interference with the rights of employees to organize, form labor organizations, bargain collectively, engage in concerted activities for the purpose of collective bargaining or other mutual aid or protection, and, also, to refrain from any of the above activities; domination of or interference with the formation or administration of a labor organization or support of a labor organization financially or otherwise; discrimination in terms of employment to either encourage or discourage membership in a labor organization; discrimination against an employee for filing charges or giving testimony under the NLRA; refusal to bargain collectively with representatives selected by a majority of employees in a bargaining unit.

Essentially, each of these employer unfair labor practices is a violation of the two-fold premise stated in the Introduction.

An unfair labor practice striker, upon unconditional application, is entitled to immediate reinstatement even if he has been permanently replaced. If the employer fails to reinstate the striker, even if it means discharging the replacement to make room, the striker will normally be entitled to back pay from the date he applied to return to work until he is reinstated.

An economic strike can be converted to an unfair labor practice strike by unlawful acts of the employer that serve to prolong the strike.

Unlawful Strikes

An unlawful strike is one that is either conducted by unlawful means or has an illegal purpose as its object. Employees engaging in such strikes are "unprotected," and, thus, may be discharged.

Examples of strikes conducted by unlawful means include partial strikes, such as working the normal shift but refusing to work overtime; "quickie" strikes, which are short walkouts that disadvantage the employer at little cost to the employees; slowdowns; sitdowns; and certain strikes not authorized by the union.

Examples of strikes for an unlawful purpose include strikes that violate the mandatory notice provisions of Section 8. (d) of the Act; strikes that in fact violate a no-strike clause of a labor contract (often a difficult question for even the Board and courts to resolve); a recognition strike by one union while the Board certification of another union is still valid; strikes to force an employer to agree to "featherbedding" (pay for services not performed, especially the hiring of unnecessary employees); and jurisdictional strikes to force an employer to assign disputed work to the striking union rather than another union.

Note, however, that the Board and courts have carved out certain exceptions to the general rules defining unprotected strikes. Therefore, if you think you are the victim of such a strike, do not start discharging everyone in sight until you have checked with your legal counsel.

Keep in mind, too, that any striker guilty of illegal misconduct associated with the strike (another difficult issue many times) can be discharged. This includes strikers participating in any kind of strike.

You can see, then, that before you take on a strike, it is imperative that you know, to the fullest extent possible, whether you or the union stands to win the legal battle. It is a rare and endangered breed of employer who consciously enters the fray against a band of strikers who have nothing to lose.

Implementing a Strike Response

Generally speaking, it should take about four weeks to get a strike response operation in order, and that should be true for a small or large organization. Of course, just reading this manual will provide some useful insights, but to get prepared takes time.

Just to have a framework as reference, let us assume there are 800 persons in your employ. Three hundred are in your production unit and represented by a union. The collective bargaining agreement expired three weeks ago; you have been in contract negotiations about ten weeks. There are a few noneconomic demands unsettled, but the big unresolved issue is wages. You have offered a seven percent increase; the union wants ten.

Fifty employees are in the maintenance unit, represented by another union. The contract is not open for several months; it contains a no-strike clause.

The other 450 employees are nonrepresented office and clerical, including a security force of twenty.

You believe that unless the company meets the union's wage demand there will be a strike. You believe the demand is too high and that your wage proposal is fair and reasonable. You feel the company should stand its ground and that the plant should continue operations if a strike should occur. Top management has been advised and agrees. It is time to act.

The first and most critical step in the establishment of your entire strike response is the appointment by the chief executive officer of one person to be in charge. This person, as Emergency Operations Manager, will answer only to the person who appointed him.

The emergency operations manager will chair and work through the Emergency Operations Committee (EOC), which is discussed in the next section, but his authority is paramount. If the committee members disagree among themselves or with him, he prevails. If a decision must be made between committee meetings, it is his decision to make.

He can spend company funds, transfer employees, appoint assistants to himself, establish other committees, hire additional plant security—in short, take any reasonable action to assist the strike defense effort.

And he can act without going through channels. If he says do it, it is to be done. The paperwork can be filled out after the strike is won.

His role and authority are crucial. Without this person as "CEO" of the entire strike operation, it is likely that the attitude among your managers will be "someone else is supposed to do that." The end result will be that strike preparations are neither diligently pursued nor effectively implemented.

The person to handle this critical task must be carefully selected. His regular position should be high on the organization chart. More important than his background (Production, Personnel, whatever—he will seek out the advice he needs) is the individual himself. He must be well known and respected for his abilities, persuasive, tactful, creative, organized, and tireless. He must exhort maximum effort from others while maintaining peace in the corporate family. He must be a leader.

His appointment, the reason for it, and a tactful summary of his authority are announced by the CEO in a confidential memo to all vice-presidents and department heads. See Exhibit 1 for a sample memo.

Hereafter, the manual is written as if you have been selected and announced.

The Emergency Operations Committee

The Emergency Operations Committee (EOC) will include all department heads (several of whom will serve on one of the other committees you will create). In our hypothetical company this means 15 to 20 persons: the head of Personnel, Sales, Accounting, Purchasing, Promotion, Engineering, Production, etc. In addition, all vice-presidents are invited to attend committee meetings, without necessarily being named as members. You can decide this based on your feel for the organization. Of course, if a vice-president is head of a department, he should be an EOC member.

If your company has a large enough boardroom, use it for EOC meetings. It will properly enhance the importance of the committee.

Set the first EOC meeting for about the fifth working day following your appointment. In your memo (see Exhibit 2) calling the meeting, give the time and place, of course, and state in general what is to be covered. The agenda will include a review of contract negotiations, the company's position in the bargaining, the functions of the committee, and the formation of certain smaller, specialized committees. Emphasize that attendance is imperative.

Prepare a questionnaire to be distributed to each EOC member at the first meeting and returned at the second. When answered, each questionnaire will serve as the basis for a "department" strike plan. Exhibit 3 is an example of such a questionnaire.

Arrange for your chief labor negotiator to present a review of and outlook for the contract negotiations. He must clearly define the major differences between the parties and stress the validity of the company's unwillingness to change its position on the crucial wage issue. He must be certain to ensure that the committee members understand the issues and that the company's offer is fair. It is important, obviously, that the committee members believe in the cause. Accurately presented, they

11

will. This portion of the meeting, with time for questions, can easily take an hour.

Arrange for the CEO to introduce you and remain in attendance. It is not necessary that he attend later meetings, though he may well choose to.

Appoint a noncommittee member to take, transcribe, and distribute minutes of this and each subsequent meeting. Copies go to all members plus all vice-presidents and the CEO.

That takes care of the procedural arrangements for the first EOC meeting. Your real work, the work that wins strikes, begins before the EOC meets. Your most important pre-EOC step is the selection of three special committees. Use your best judgment; these are the people who will count most in preparing for and combating the strike.

These special committees are described below.

Production Committee

Include the key people directly involved in manufacturing the product(s): the Production manager, the head of each sub-department within Production, and the heads of Engineering, Maintenance, Inspection, Purchasing, and Shipping and Receiving. Also name a sharp individual from Sales to serve as liasion between your customers, the front office, and the "shop."

Production Support Committee

Include on this committee key persons from departments that assist the production process, for example, Security, Employment, Labor Relations, Training, Safety, Wage and Salary Administration, Payroll, and perhaps Data Processing and Accounting.

Strike Control Center

Select a strong personality not included on either of the other special committees. His staff can be drawn from his own and other departments. Unlike the first two special committees, the strike control group serves in a comprehensive information processing and "strike action" role. Much more about that later.

Personally notify the persons selected to serve on these committees, and name the chairman of each. You will meet with these committees separately after the first Emergency Operations Committee meeting.

The Emergency Operations Committee Meets

The first meeting of the EOC will be used, in addition to the reasons stated earlier, to establish a sense of teamwork, urgency, and the importance of the committee to the strike response. This committee is important, of course, but probably not so much for what it does as for what it represents. You will find, for instance, that a substantial number of members and their departments will contribute little beyond continuing normal operations and loaning a few employees to other areas. This is certainly important, and necessary, but even more valuable to the company's overall effort is the fact that the managers of these departments are aware of the mechanics of the strike response and feel an integral part of it. So be sure this committee continues to meet regularly, at least once a week to begin with and more often as the strike appears imminent.

The CEO introduces you, and you make a few remarks to set the scene, such as:

Gentlemen, thank you for coming. This strike business is a new experience for us, and we are in for some hard work.

We are in the right in these negotiations, and it looks like we may have to take on a walk-out to prove it. We are willing to do that....and we'll come out on top. I can't tell you it will be easy, but I know it will be worth it.

For those of you who don't already know, the big issue in these negotiations is money. The union is insisting on a ten percent increase across the board; we are offering seven. And seven is as high as we intend to go. If that means we get struck then so be it. We are not going to grant a wage increase that will price our product out of the market. I know all of you will agree with that.

Anyway, we have a lot of ground to cover this morning. I have a lot to discuss with you, and I need to know your thinking.

We will be working together closely these next few weeks.

I know some of you are not entirely familiar with the circumstances that have brought us together today, so, I have asked Mr.

_____, the head of our contract bargaining team, to review the negotiations for us and tell us what he foresees down the line. He will also sit in on our future meetings to keep us as current as possible. Mr._____. . . .

After he speaks and answers questions, you continue:

Gentlemen, if the union strikes us, there is going to be a lot happening at once. We cannot get ready for the strike after it happens. We must do it now.

If the company is to be prepared, each department must be prepared. Therefore, at the close of the meeting each of you will receive a questionnaire to be completed and returned to me at our next meeting. If you have any questions about how to fill it out ask them before we leave or give me a call later.

This committee will serve in an overall coordinating capacity. We will meet regularly until it appears the strike is upon us. Then we will meet daily, or more often, for as long as necessary.

I have appointed three special committees to begin work immediately. The primary function of the first, Production, is just that, to maintain our production level as near normal as we can manage. The second, Production Support, will provide assistance to the production effort. The third will operate the Strike Control Center and will be charged with providing us current information on all aspects of the strike, both internally and externally, It will also serve as the action center for strike response activities.

Announce the members and chairman of each special committee and that each will hold its initial meeting prior to the second EOC session.

Close with a question and answer period. This should be included in the minutes. Try to get the answers to all questions and consult other committee members and legal counsel if necessary. Include these as a part of the minutes. You can conclude with:

"Our next meeting is set for (a week later) here in this room. I will report to you on the progress of the other committees at that time, and we will be updated on the negotiations. I will also be looking forward to receiving the completed questionnaires. If you have questions or ideas in the meantime, let me know.

The Special Committees Meet

Meet with one committee each day, beginning the day after the first EOC meeting.

Try to impress on each of the three committees the importance of its work and the seriousness with which it must be undertaken. Each committee member must do his work with utmost thoroughness if the operation is to be successful. Indicate also that each committee's role, while an integral part of the whole, cannot be performed or "covered" by the work of another committee. If a committee fails, the operation fails.

It is your job to get each committee going. When you first meet with a committee it is likely none of its members will have any real idea of what is to be done. Start slowly; paint the big picture and then focus on the details. The important thing is to get the committee members thinking. It is probably correct that finding the right questions is harder than their answers.

By the way, it is recommended that you have a stenographer keep minutes of each of these committee's meetings, if for no one else, for you.

Following are some questions and thoughts for each committee. You will no doubt think of many others, as will the committee members. You will find that implementing the answers to some questions will be the responsibility of a committee other than the committee that raised and answered them. For instance, Production Support will be responsible for recruiting the employees the Production Committee determines it needs. This situation will require intercommittee communication. While such communication will largely be the responsibility of the Strike Control Center Committee, it would be well to appoint an assistant to yourself to coordinate such matters. Have him attend all committee meetings with you.

15

Production Committee

Obviously, the Production Committee must concentrate on keeping the lines moving. What is actually involved and where do you start? What are the needs in terms of people, materials, and equipment and from where will they come? Try to get the committee members to visualize the company's production needs generally and then focus on the details. Have them assume no production workers will show for work tomorrow. What would happen? Then, in detail, what must happen if the product is to be produced? Do the same exercise for materials.

In getting down to details, approach the requirements of production from two viewpoints: (a) the *process* of production, beginning with purchasing and ending with shipping; and (b) the *people* who will produce: who will they be, where will they come from, what can they do.

The Process of Production

Purchasing, of course, must continue to supply the production units with the materials necessary to continue operations.

Each vendor should be informed of the pending strike situation and his assistance solicited in making deliveries as you need them. Contact not just the salesman you normally deal with, but the general manager as well. Try to get specific commitments from each supplier and keep records of your contacts. When completed, the form, as exemplified by Exhibit 4, will enable you to make a reasonable estimate of deliveries you can expect from each vendor.

Does each vendor understand his obligation to make deliveries in spite of picket lines? Be sure he does, but be tactful. Interstate Commerce Commission regulations require truckers and railroads—common carriers—to continue deliveries except in limited instances in which the driver reasonably fears bodily harm. Consider also arranging with each vendor to make quick deliveries when your entrances are temporarily without pickets, or to have his supervisors drive the trucks through the line.

Consider establishing an offsite delivery point. (If all else fails, company trucks manned by nonunion personnel can pick up shipments away from the plant and bring them across the picket line.) Where should it be located? What advance arrangements need to be made? Use of a form such as Exhibit 5 will help.

Decide what materials should be stockpiled in advance. In what quantity? And where? Will an offsite warehouse be required? For material stockpiling, use the form shown in Exhibit 6. For investigating offsite warehouse locations, consult Exhibit 7.

Discuss the problems that may arise if material orders will need to be revised to fit adjusted production schedules.

At a later meeting, after the above has been completed, estimate as best you can your material status on the first, second, third, etc., day(s) of the strike. Use Exhibit 8 for this. Ideally, you should be ready to make this estimate at the second meeting of this committee.

Maintenance and protection of plant equipment is vital.

A schedule should be prepared for performing needed maintenance *now*, before the strike. Do now what you have been putting off. See Exhibit 9.

How will idle equipment be stored or otherwise protected from sabotage? Consult Exhibit 10.

Vulnerable areas such as generator and transformer rooms must be secured. Use Exhibit 11 to develop your plan.

Someone should screen maintenance work orders and investigate machinery breakdowns for signs of tampering.

All production foremen should be advised that during the strike they will be responsible for the safekeeping of all company hand tools, ensuring that all unattended power equipment is shut down, and for making frequent machinery safety inspections of their respective units.

Can you determine what repairs and/or installations can be reduced in scope or postponed if it is seen that available employees are needed elsewhere? (No doubt the CEO can do without that shower for his office until after the strike.)

Delivery of the product requires similar considerations as receipt of materials. Arrange to make all possible shipments prior to the strike. Find out if some customers will accept larger than usual orders to build up their inventories. Use Exhibit 12 for this.

Have you informed current shippers of the pending strike and obtained their assurance that pick-ups will continue as needed? Find out their status with a form such as Exhibit 13.

Use Exhibit 14 to arrange for nonunion shippers to step in if necessary.

Have you devised a plan to supply customers on a pro rata basis if your production is reduced once the strike begins? Exhibit 15 elicits information that will help you create a workable plan for this.

Subcontracting may be necessary. It seems clear that a company can legally subcontract during a strike in order to maintain production—and do so without notifying or bargaining with the union. Beyond that, such as permanently subcontracting work (and thereby eliminating bargaining unit jobs), there are pitfalls. It can be legally accomplished, however, if you can show legitimate and substantial business reasons for it. This is a complex area, so consult your counsel before you subcontract. However, you should contact and make tentative arrangements with firms that can do the work for you in case you do decide to "farm out" certain functions. Have the Production Committee provide the information requested in Exhibit 16.

The People for Production

Have you obtained from each foreman his estimate of which of his employees will continue to work during the strike? At least a few will, even if they have to run over picketing unionists to get into the plant. The foreman's estimate is likely to be fairly accurate. Each foreman should be instructed to prepare such a prediction now, by employee name and job skills. He should be conservative, of course; it will not adversely reflect on him if he thinks only two of fifty will show. Each foreman should also furnish the number of employees by skills he will need to maintain various levels of production. Exhibit 17 will assist him in making these estimates.

Based on these evaluations, use Exhibit 18 to prepare an overall estimate of strike production capabilities from the personnel standpoint. With this you will be in a much better position to estimate how many employees need to be recruited and/or transferred and what skills they must have.

Determine which Production department staff employees can be shifted to production work. Many of these people will have retained their mechanical skills. Inventory these people and what they can do by using Exhibit 19.

Make arrangements to obtain from the Production Support Committee the names of office employees who can be released. Again, some of these people will have valuable production skills. Those who do not can be quickly trained to do simple production, inspection, production clerical tasks, timekeeping, clean up, and certain maintenance. This should free a few higher skilled workers who are needed elsewhere.

(Note: Get a reading on the Fair Labor Standards Act overtime requirements for these employees. Persons who are in exempt jobs may lose their exempt status during weeks they perform production work; if that happens, they must be paid overtime for hours worked in excess of forty per workweek. Other FLSA hourly rate/overtime problems may arise in the case of non-exempt employees who split their workweeks between their regular job—at one hourly rate—and a production job at a different hourly rate. These problems are often complicated and merit your close attention.)

Based on your foremen's estimates and your evaluation of how much help you can expect from transferred employees, you should have a reasonably good idea of what your new hire requirements will be. Bear in mind, of course, that the reinstatement rights of economic strikers are not affected by *temporary* replacements. If your strategy is not to rehire strikers, then you will want to recruit heavily (but selectively) for permanent new employees, and you can anticipate that your office-to-plant employee transfers will be for less than the duration of the strike. This does not mean that you cannot *permanently* transfer employees into the jobs affected by the walk-out. You can. Normally, you do not.

By using Exhibits 8 and 18, the Production Committee should be able to prepare fairly accurate estimates of your company's production capabilities. These estimates will also help you know where your efforts need to be directed. For instance, assume it is estimated that (a) personnel are available to maintain 85% of normal production with no overtime and 100% by working six 8-hour days, and (b) only 80% of normal material deliveries will be received the first week of the strike. Obviously, then, you know you need to concentrate your efforts toward increasing the flow of materials into the plant, and you would likely have no reason to authorize overtime until the shortage is corrected.

Again, these estimates must be updated frequently. The material/personnel relationships can change quickly and you must be kept aware of these changes as they occur.

Production Support Committee

This committee will have responsibility for four basic areas: employment and training; "plant" labor relations (as opposed to collective bargaining, unfair labor practice charges and the like); security; and plant services.

Employment and Training

Prepare a list of all nonbargaining unit employees indicating alternate skills, present job and department, shift, extension, and home telephone and address. If all this information is not available in Personnel it can be obtained from the various department heads. Use Exhibit 20.

Prepare newspaper, radio, and other help wanted advertisements for striker replacements. You can legally state that a labor dispute is in progress and that you have permanent positions available. If considerable overtime is anticipated, say so in your ad if you want to. For example, "$1000+ per week with overtime" may well draw in some good people; the disadvantage is they may leave when the overtime plays out and thereby "reopen" the jobs of some strikers. You will have to balance your production needs with your desire to truly permanently replace the strikers. Note: Some states have laws that require ads such as you will be running to indicate that a strike is in progress. Check this. And see Exhibit 21 for some sample ads.

Contact applicant referral sources, such as employment agencies, trade schools, and community organizations, to let them know you may need a lot of people in a hurry. Note: Your local office of the state employment commission is precluded by law from referring applicants to replace strikers.

Have Personnel contact friends at other companies regarding the referral to you of applicants they do not need but you do. Personnel can also find out if any comparable industries in your area and elsewhere have employees on lay off; the names, skills, and addresses of these employees may be made available to you. Perhaps before, but certainly after the strike occurs, they can be contacted about coming to work for you. There is the disadvantage that they may leave if recalled by their former employer. Again, it is the question to what extent you can afford to seek only those new hires most likely to be permanent.

Consider interviewing and "hiring" applicants on an "if we need you" basis. However, do not flaunt this sort of preparation. It is fine to be ready for a walk-out but not to be showy about the fact that you are getting ready. Such showmanship may be considered an unfair labor practice, as, for example, in the case of parading a group of applicants through the plant when this is not normal practice. Such action on your part may be found to be an unlawful attempt to "chill" the aspirations of would-be strike participants. See Exhibit 22 for an applicant record form.

And lest you forget: Strike replacements cannot be offered a higher base wage than was offered the strikers. This does not, of course, preclude replacements from working any and all the overtime you see fit to authorize.

Arrange for any necessary training for new and current employees. Can you predict what kinds of training will be required? Where and by whom will it be taught? How long should it take? You should be able to come up with a reasonable estimate of training needs based on Exhibits 18, 19, and 20. Use Exhibit 23 to set up your training program. Of course, any training you conduct should be on company time—in other words, paid.

Be prepared to keep your personnel office open longer hours, and on Saturday and Sunday if need be.

Prepare a listing of available housing to assist new hires from out of town. Contact apartment owners, boarding houses, the "Y," and others. Use Exhibit 24.

Have on hand a supply of city maps, bus route schedules, and commercial parking lot locations (near the plant) for these out-of-city new people.

Be ready to issue "final" paychecks to the strikers on the payday next following the walkout. Do not call them "final" checks; you do not want to cause the strikers to think they are being discharged. If a striker has accrued vacation which by contract or company policy he is entitled to take or be paid for whether or not he ever returns to work, it would be well to pay him for it if he so requests. In fact, you may want to offer to pay him for it, if for no other reason than to give him one less opportunity to contact you later. See Exhibit 25.

Arrange to discontinue paying the premiums on group insurance and other fringe benefits for strikers. You can legally cease such payments unless you are contractually obligated otherwise, and this is unlikely. You are not, after all, required to financially support the strike. And see that your people who handle claims are on the lookout for any that the strikers may submit. Unless these claims are the result of occurrences for which the premium was paid previously, they should be denied.

Notify the state employment commission of the strike on the day it takes place. In many states strikers are not eligible for unemployment compensation, so send the local office a list of the names, addresses, and social security numbers of the strikers. And be sure to protest any such claims that are filed, including attending any hearings the commission may hold.

Stockpile medical supplies. Have First Aid order a three-month supply of everything you normally keep on hand. Notify one or more ambulance services of the pending strike. Let them know you will be counting on them for extra efficient service; give them clear directions to the plant and the entrance to use, as well as the hospital you want to handle your cases.

Arrange for round-the-clock first aid. If your present staff is not large enough to provide it, employ nurses on a temporary basis from your local medical bureau. And ensure in advance that only nurses who will cross picket lines will be referred to you.

Plant Labor Relations

You may have foremen who are still members of the union. This often happens when an employee is promoted to supervisor and does not drop his membership. If you have supervisors in this category, instruct them (diplomatically at first, emphatically later if necessary) to resign from the union before the strike. So long as your foremen are in fact supervisors under the NLRA you can legally require them to get out of the union. If they do not resign and subsequently perform bargaining unit work during the strike, their union can fine them heavily and the courts will uphold it. The word "foreman" should be taken to mean all supervisors as defined in the Act, regardless of title.

Obviously, it is important that you know which of your foremen are by law supervisors. It is, after all, one thing to require a supervisor to drop his union card and quite another to demand it of an employee. The distinction is not always easily made, since the line between supervisor and "leadman" or "straw boss" is often fuzzy. Job titles are not much help; actual authority and responsibility are the determining factors.

The Act provides that supervisors are persons who have the authority to do one or more of the following: hire; transfer; suspend; lay off; recall; promote; discharge; assign; reward; discipline; direct; and adjust grievances—or to effectively recommend such action.

In practice, you will have an easier time establishing that an employee is a supervisor if he has in fact exercised his authority by actually hiring, disciplining, promoting, etc. In any event, before you suggest to a "borderline" supervisor that he drop his card, have the circumstances of his particular case reviewed by counsel. If you do not, and it turns out you have required an employee (not a supervisor) to resign from the union, you have violated the Act. You do not want that to happen, particularly now.

Arrange to conduct "strike training" for all your foremen. This is of vital importance for several reasons. For one thing, you want to ensure that your foremen know they are part of the management team; in addition, they certainly will want to be kept informed about the strike situation, and they should be. But perhaps most important is the fact that as representatives (legally, agents) of management, the manner in which your foremen conduct themselves before and during the strike can measurably assist your strike response, or literally destroy it.

It is unlawful, for instance, for a foreman to make a statement to employees that gives the impression of intended interference with their rights (including the right to strike) or of discrimination between union members and nonmembers, strikers and nonstrikers. Thus, a foreman's well intended but "unlawful" statement to employees can convert what would have been (or otherwise was) an economic strike into an unfair labor practice strike.

Your foreman training should take place early in your strike preparations. These training sessions are also an opportune time to update your foremen on the labor situation and get their frequently valuable feedback.

You should meet with about ten foremen each session, and meet with each group at least three times, several days apart. And because you do not want any of them worrying about making a unit deadline and not listening to you, hold your meetings at "slack" times for them. A couple of hours into the shift is usually good. Use Exhibit 26 to schedule your foreman training.

In spite of the gravity of the matters you will discuss, do not make the mistake of frightening your foremen into thinking they cannot say anything to their employees without breaking the law. What each must avoid, put simply, is making statements that sound like threats of reprisal (if the employee strikes) or promises of benefit (if he does not strike). On the other hand, the Act does not preclude the expression of any views, argument, or opinion, provided, of course, neither threat nor promise of benefit is present.

The following are some examples of improper and proper comments:

"Say, Joe, come here a minute. I hear the union had a meeting last night to take a strike vote. I hope you weren't crazy enough to vote for it." There is the threat of reprisal here, somewhat subtle. In effect, if you had to be crazy to vote for a strike, it could mean the company will be out to get you if you did. If not, why did the foreman want to know how the employee voted, or even that he attended the meeting? There is no valid reason for the foreman to make such a statement.

"I don't know for sure, Tom, and I can't promise anything, but I hear the people who stay with the company are going to be a little better off after the strike." This "non-promise" might persuade Tom not to strike—illegally.

"You guys can strike if you want to, but don't be standing in the street when I drive up. I might not see you." It is doubtful that even the dullest employee would interpret this remark as concern for his safety.

"What you people decide about this strike thing is your business. As far as I can see, it doesn't make sense. You'll be out of work and you could be permanently replaced." This seems to be a perfectly legal expression of opinion and fact.

"I'll say this. The company has a lot of friends around here, and I'll bet none of them will hire anyone out on strike if the company puts the word out." Had the statement ended after "strike," it would arguably be a statement of opinion and no more. As it is, however, there is clearly a threat of reprisal.

"No, I don't think you should strike. Some of you could lose your homes and cars if it lasted very long, and I'd hate to see that happen. Besides, I don't think the company's offer is all that bad." This comment looks to be an honest, nonthreatening statement of opinion, and acceptable.

Suppose the foreman had added, "And what's more, I don't think a strike will change the company's mind." This addition does not appear to change the tenor of the statement.

But suppose the foreman had added instead, "And besides that, if you strike, the company just might shut this place down and move to Florida." This might not be illegal if it could be established that it was intended as a joke among friends and was so taken. However, a brewing strike is not a joking matter. Avoid this sort of comment.

"Look, fellows, the company is trying to reach an agreement and will keep on trying even if you walk out. I really don't think your going on strike is going to speed up these negotiations or cause the company to give in. The truth is the company feels that what it is offering is fair, and there's no law that says the company has to meet the union's demands. I really hope none of you will walk out if and when the union calls a strike." Again, here is presented honest opinion and fact without threat or promise.

"The union you belong to has been engaged in a lot of strikes over the years, and I'll bet if you compare their gains and their losses, you'd see your chances of getting what you want aren't that great." This is probably okay, although the foreman seems to be basing his opinions on other opinions. What is "a lot of strikes" and over how many years? Has he compared gains and losses? How does he compute "chances?" This sort of comment points up the need for you to furnish your foremen some *facts* about the union and particularly its strike history, if it has been less than successful. This information can be obtained from the trade or industry association your company belongs to or your state association of business. It would have been much more meaningful if the foreman could have truthfully stated, "In the past ten years this union has called 22 strikes nationwide and as a result about 1200 people were replaced and lost their jobs."

"Yes, Alice, it's true the company is making some preparations to keep operating in case the union calls a strike. In my opinion, we'll keep the lines moving even if everyone the union represents walks out. That doesn't mean we want a strike, we don't. But it does mean we don't intend to let a strike shut us down." This statement combines fact and noncoercive opinion and should be safe. Of course, the fact in the statement is not one that the foreman should go around flaunting, but if inquiry is made of him, there is no reason for him not to tell the truth.

"Look, Bill, this company has paid good wages for many years. You may not think so, but I do. And we both know the benefits are great. How are you going to feel if you go on strike knowing you won't have any group insurance? It would scare me, I guarantee you that. I hope you'll think about that before you do something you might regret." This appears to be free of either threat of reprisal or promise of benefit. It also points up the need for your foremen to have some wage and benefit information they can pass along if the occasion arises. Your foremen should know how your pay scales and fringes compare to other industries in the area and how much your company pays in benefits for each dollar paid in wages. Then the foreman could say: "Look, Bill, the company already pays about 18¢ an hour more than most companies around here, and we've offered a 7% increase. Besides that, we're one of very few companies I know of that pays 90% of the group insurance premium, and that costs the company about 80 bucks a month for each employee. We've got very good benefits, they should be, they cost the company about 40¢ for every dollar that goes to wages."

"I think if it weren't for the union, the company would be paying 50¢ an hour more." This may be honest opinion, but it is not a bright statement to make. There is assuredly no basis in fact for such a comment, but a not-so-bright employee might be influenced by it to quit the union, and that is a dangerous result.

"Kathy, I understand there may be a strike tomorrow. I need to know how many people I'll have because I'm going to try to get some work out. Will you be here?" This is not recommended. It is not certain there will be a strike tomorrow, or even that there will be a strike at all, and Kathy might feel that the foreman is making a list of everyone who *would* have struck if they had had the chance. However, if the union *announces* a strike or it is otherwise known when the strike is going to start, the foreman should be safe in making the inquiry. In neither case would it be permissible to add something like, "I'll make it worth your while to come in."

"Jerry, I saw you give this leaflet to Louis, and I want you to stop handing them out. Next time it happens you'll get a formal warning." If the foreman has a long-standing, well-enforced rule against distributting literature, well and good. If he does not, however, his statement to Jerry, even if devoid of antiunion animus, is dangerous. It makes no sense to start enforcing previously unenforced rules (much less promulgate new ones) simply because a strike is brewing. On the other hand, there is no call to relax objective, even-handed discipline. It should be business as usual.

Notwithstanding the foregoing, the fact remains that a given statement can be found to be illegal in one circumstance and legal in another. The National Labor Relations Board is perfectly willing to delve into attendant factors, such as the relationship between the foreman and the employee, other statements made by the foreman, the strike "atmosphere" in the plant at the time, and the employee's reaction to the statement in order to determine its status. Do not, of course, take this to mean that any statement can be "saved" by an investigation of the circumstances surrounding it; clear threats and clear promises are doomed.

Therefore, while the above examples should help your foremen negotiate the thin line between statements the Board will and will not condone, they should be instructed above all to use tact, discretion, and sound judgment in making any strike-related comment.

Again, these examples also point up the need for you to provide your foremen with certain information regarding the company and the union. These include:

1. *Facts* about the union's strike history and about the wages and benefits of your company in relation to the local market and comparable industries. The Personnel office should have or be able to quickly obtain this data.

2. *Facts* about collective bargaining. Your chief labor negotiator can no doubt work something up on short notice. Your foremen should know, for example:

   •The company is required by law to bargain in good faith with the union regarding wages, hours and working conditions, but the company is not required by law to agree to a union proposal or to make a concession.
   •A union cannot require an employer to give more than the employer is willing to give.
   •Economic strikers can be permanently replaced.
   •The company is not bound to continue making premium payments for fringe benefits during a strike.
   •The union cannot guarantee that the employees will gain any-

thing by going on strike—not higher wages, not better benefits, not job security, not anything.

3. *Facts* about the current negotiations—what the unresolved issues are and each party's position on them, the issues that have already been settled and what the company has agreed to give.

One last word about foreman statements: Be sure to tell each foreman that if he is asked a question he does not know the answer to, to say so, and tell the employee he will get the answer and get back with him. Foremen should not feel they must appear to know everything. (In fact, no one on the strike team should, not even the Emergency Operations Manager.)

It would be well during these meetings to emphasize to your foremen that you consider them an integral part of the management team. Stress to them that the success of the strike response depends in large measure on their efforts. It is the truth, and your foremen should know it.

By the same token, your foremen are agents of the company. By and large, what they say is imputed to their employer, and the company is held accountable for it. Therefore, if a foreman errs, you must act quickly to rectify the mistake. First, disavow the statement publicly and assure the employees the statement was made in error and does not reflect company policy or intent. Talk directly to the employees to whom the statement was made and ask the shop steward to be present. If what was said has gotten spread around the shop, use notices on bulletin boards or even call a meeting of all employees to disavow and reassure. And if you feel the statement was made more in bad faith than in error, discipline the foreman. In any event, advise your counsel of the incident immediately.

Regarding a related matter, arrange for a member of your labor relations staff to review or, even better, be consulted in advance of all plant disciplinary action. It will be his responsibility to preclude the occurrence of discrimination against known pro-strike employees. It will not do, for instance, to give the pro-strike employee three days off for an offense for which a "company" employee gets a verbal warning. In fact, if such action should initiate the strike, it would likely be an unfair labor practice strike. And, similarly, if such discriminatory treatment should somehow occur during a strike, it might well convert it from an economic to an unfair labor practice strike.

Finally, consider how you will handle grievances arising during the strike. (Until and unless legally ousted, the union continues to represent bargaining unit employees even though most of them are replacements.) If you intend to significantly alter the procedure in effect prior to the strike, the union must be given the opportunity to bargain about the changes. Arbitration is an exception; because the duty to arbitrate terminates with the contract, you can refuse to arbitrate grievances that arise following the expiration of the labor agreement.

Security

You will utilize your present security force and, if advisable, employ contract guards. Many companies furnishing such personnel are experienced in working strikes and can provide a trained and competent force. Contact several such companies and compare their costs and what they have to offer. Use the form outlined in Exhibit 27. The prospects of violence by the strikers, the size, experience, and loyalty of your own security force, and the benefits to employee morale are among the factors you should consider in determining whether or not to engage a security contractor. Bear in mind, however, that the safety of your employees, plant, and equipment is of major importance. If you have the slightest doubt that your current security department is ready, willing, and able, then by all means contract for the help you need. And do so in a timely fashion—before a warehouse burns.

Arrange to make ID badges for all employees. Show the employee's name, department, social security number, and photograph on the badge. The badges should be prepared in advance of the strike and issued before or as soon as the strike begins. The badges should be considered a valid security measure and therefore prepared for the potential strikers as well as the other employees. Just do not use them as a scare tactic. The equipment needed to produce these badges can be rented.

Work out a revised work schedule for the Security department employees to maximize the available force. This may include longer shifts, six or seven-day workweeks, and canceled vacations. See Exhibit 28. Preparing this schedule may help you decide whether or not you need to contract for outside security help. If you decide to hire outside assistance, arrange the work schedule of your own employees so that they are spread thinly among the posts to be manned. It will be helpful to the outside security guards to be working alongside someone who is familiar with the facility and your employees.

Arrange to meet with city, county, and state law enforcement officials to obtain their assurances of fast response time if an emergency situation arises. They will appreciate and be flattered by your talking with them in advance. Follow up each visit with a letter thanking them for their time and expressing your complete confidence in the agency they represent. You should also notify all federal and state agencies with whom the company does business, and the FBI and railroad police if tracks enter your property. Use Exhibit 29 to record all such meetings.

Arrange for secure transportation to and from work for threatened employees. This might be by way of leased vans and buses or security escort of employee cars. It might also be worthwhile to use your personnel records to determine where clusters of your employees live. Such employees might want to meet at a central point and drive to work in a caravan or, if some can leave their cars where they meet, car pool. They might feel more comfortable commuting this way, particularly if picket line disturbances are anticipated.

The homes of some employees and executives may draw the attention of strikers; vandalism is a real possibility. Be prepared to provide 24-hour guard service for the residence of each such individual.

Have you investigated furnishing a two-way radio for each guard on duty? This can certainly reduce response time in an emergency, and one such occasion will more than justify the cost.

Prepare small maps of the plant for each guard showing important locations (entrances to the facility, transformers, docks, etc.) for faster response by security personnel who are not familiar with the entire plant.

Establish guard stations inside all building entrances to inspect packages brought in or taken out by employees, the employees of subcontractors and suppliers, and the public. Your guards must, of course, use discretion and tact in handling this assignment. Unless the strike is particularly bitter and you legitimately fear something like arson or the theft of essential machine parts, there is no real need to frisk everyone who walks by. In fact, it is probably deterent enough to have a guard seated at a desk on which you have placed a sign reading: "Packages carried by persons entering or leaving this building are subject to examination."

Seriously investigate the need for additional lighting of areas such as plant entrances, isolated buildings, perimeter fencing, and, of utmost importance, company parking lots. A striker desiring to sneak onto your property to slash tires or worse, is much less likely to do so if he must first pass under bright lights. Your employees will also feel safer walking to their cars.

Speaking of fencing, be sure that what is already in place is in good repair. It should be at least six feet high and topped by barbed wire. Install new fences where you have unprotected property lines. And be sure to arrange for Security to check all your fencing every morning and evening.

Establish a plan for the location of your guard force during the strike. (As already mentioned, if you use outside personnel you will want your own security employees spread thinly among the posts to be manned.) But determine also how many guards will be stationed at each post. For instance, you may initially want at least three near each entrance, one atop each building, two in each warehouse, two or three in each production area, two patrolling the parking lots, several "on call" in the security office, and so on. (Again, if you decide to utilize the assistance of outside security, that firm's "strike captain" can help you with this if he is called in early in your preparations.) Naturally, whatever format you develop now will likely change as the strike proceeds, but you need to have a plan ready to implement the moment the strike is initiated. Exhibit 30 will help in this regard.

Have on hand an adequate supply of binoculars and Incident Report Forms (Exhibit 31). Guards working the entrances to your plant should carry or have immediate access to small tape recorders in order to obtain graphic, word-for-word accounts of victims of or witnesses to picket line violence or other abuse.

Still and movie cameras should also be immediately available to guards who know how to use them. Any person who might use one of these cameras must fully understand he is to employ it only to record mass picketing (discussed later in the manual); violence, or the results of either such unlawful activity. Photographs or movies must not be taken of legal picketing (because it is considered by the Board to intimidate or instill in strikers a fear of reprisal) or of the distribution of literature (considered to be an infringement of the Constitutional rights of free speech).

Develop a plan for pairs of nonuniformed persons to test the picket line periodically. The purpose, of course, is to ascertain if the pickets are detering persons from entering the plant by threats or serious verbal abuse. But by all means, be certain these persons can be depended on not to reciprocate in kind. If their access onto your facility is obstructed, they should calmly and clearly request that they be permitted to enter. If the obstruction continues they should leave and immediately record all details of the encounter: the date, time, location, names or description of each picket, and everything said or done by each person involved, including the persons making the report. The Incident Report Form can be used. It should be forwarded to your legal counsel at once as the basis for an injunction against the illegal activity.

Inspect and ensure the adequacy of your present fire protection equipment. You may want to purchase additional fire extinguishers for hazardous and/or remote areas.

If you do not already have them, construct a guard shack at each vehicle entrance and employee gate. These will serve very well to store the cameras and tape recorder mentioned above. It might be well to have a fire extinguisher in each shack, too.

If there are serious legal questions involved in the strike and you consider the union somewhat "sophisticated," have all your meeting rooms inspected at frequent intervals for electronic bugging.

Have Security prepare a building and facility patrol schedule. The buildings and grounds should be checked every day, and employee parking areas every hour or so. Frequent, obvious patrols on a varying schedule will reassure your employees and help deter would-be intruders. See Exhibit 32.

Your security officers should be prepared to assist law enforcement agencies in their investigations of cases of willful damage to company property, and you must be prepared to follow through. If you are willing to file warranted complaints, you may well receive more timely, enthusiastic support from these agencies than you will if you are reluctant to give their efforts your full support. Also, if you demonstrate your willingness to take action when it is called for, the criminal activity will decrease appreciably.

It may seem too obvious, but be sure it is clearly known who is to notify the police if violence occurs. At the start of each shift one guard at each post should be given this assignment. If there is no telephone near his station, he can use his radio to call the Security dispatcher who will then make the call. The sooner the police arrive the sooner the violence ends—and the less likely that the perpetrators will have vanished.

Be sure your guards know to be on the lookout for tacks, nails, glass, and other material that the pickets may scatter across entrances to the plant. Keep such objects in containers that indicate at which entrance they were found, date and time they were removed, and the names or descriptions of the pickets stationed at the entrance at the time.

Instruct all your security personnel not to talk with pickets unless it is clearly necessary. Frivolous conversation can lead to confrontation or, also undesirable, a sense of camaraderie.

Whether or not you decide to contract for outside security assistance, consider asking your local police to train your security employees in the basics of riot and crowd control. A few hours of hands-on instruction can instill a lot of confidence.

Establish valid reasons for striking employees to enter company premises, and make arrangements accordingly. (Valid reasons might include credit union business, picking up a paycheck, cleaning out a locker, or retrieving personal hand tools.) Ideally, each striker will have an escort the entire time he is in the building. If this is not practical, the guard who grants him admittance must notify the area he will visit that he is on his way; the person notified will in turn call the guard when the striker arrives and again when he leaves. In no case should a visiting striker be permitted to linger. This is particularly true of the production area, because nonstrikers may suspect, perhaps correctly, that he is preparing a mental list of their names.

Finally, strikers-to-be who are at work when the strike occurs sometimes have a tendency to jam equipment, lose essential company-owned tools in their coat pockets, etc. Therefore, Security must be prepared to move guards into the affected area at the moment the strike is announced. Their presence will reduce the "accident" rate.

Plant Services

Set up meetings with officials of all utilities used by your company (gas, electric, water, telephone). Explain to them that you are anticipating a strike and you want their assurance of uninterrupted service. They will appreciate this notice because they may want to make arrangements to protect their equipment and fixtures located on your premises. Also, the meeting will give them time to plan for their supervisors and other nonunion personnel to handle your needs once the picket signs go up. Record your contacts on a form similar to Exhibit 29.

Consider what emergency measures you might take if an essential service is lost. This is a great opportunity for creative thinking. For instance, suppose telephone service is interrupted. How will in-plant communications be maintained? Two-way radios might suffice, as might people assigned to do nothing except carry messages. Or do you have an internal public address system? Perhaps now is a good time to have one installed. How about outside calls you need to make? You just might send several CBers home and have a "good buddy" at the plant radio them who to call and what to say. Incoming calls? Why not arrange now with an answering service to accept your calls? Then notify everyone likely to call you to call that answering service if they cannot get through to the plant. As soon as the phones go out, you send one or more persons to the answering service to receive calls. They might also be CBers and thus could send the message on to the plant.

Can water be trucked in and portable restrooms be used if water service is lost? Generators can be leased to provide at least some of your electrical needs if necessary; possibly you can use fuel oil for heating. Determine the minimum needs of production and see if you can devise a way to meet them using alternate, emergency means. Find out what firms can bring in water (ask a fire department official what he would do), lease radios (how about a large electronics supplier?), have generators available (check with the power company and large electrical contractors), and so forth, and solicit their ideas. Use Exhibit 33 to gather your data.

Arrange to meet with the appropriate city officials for their assurance of continued trash pickups. You may want to talk with an independent trash hauler who could serve as a backup in case the city falters. Record these contacts on a form similar to Exhibit 29.

Are you prepared for employees to eat and sleep in the plant if their safety or production needs require it?

Where will they sleep—and on what? An auditorium makes a fine dormitory. If you do not have an auditorium, find out which offices can have their desks replaced with beds. Or maybe there will be some unused space in one of your warehouses. Talk with several rental agencies about their furnishing you with cots, sheets, blankets, and pillows. You might also want to consider renting TV sets, ping pong tables, and games to be set up away from the sleeping areas. Use Exhibit 34 for such information.

If your workers are "living in," you will also need to arrange for food and the means by which to prepare it. If you have a company cafeteria you should be in good shape. If not, you might contract with a local food caterer to bring in, say, one big meal during each shift. For the other meals, lay in a supply of easy-to-prepare foods—canned meats, vegetables, and fruit, instant puddings, crackers, soups, bread, and plenty of bacon, eggs, and milk. And do not forget the salt, pepper, and butter. To prepare it, you can rent cooking units and pots and pans. Of course, you will also need a can opener, and to consume this fine spread and clean up after yourself, plates, silverware, cups, napkins, dish soap and towels. Nothing to it, really. See Exhibit 35.

Establish a schedule by which your telephone switchboard will be open around the clock. And, with the help of the telephone company, develop measures to counteract attempts to jam the switchboard with a flood of calls.

Inventory your present supplies and arrange to have on hand capacity stocks of such materials as paper, typewriter ribbons, pens, other office supplies, soap, toilet paper, shop towels, print shop supplies, and all the other daily necessities you can think of. Use Exhibit 36 to keep track.

Strike Control Center Committee

This is the information, logistics, and in many respects the focal point of the entire strike operation. Open around the clock, the center gathers, releases, and acts on strike data.

The control center must be in a position to answer (or rapidly get the answer to) any strike-related question posed by a department head, foreman, or other employee who has a need to know. For example, the center should be able to respond to a night foreman who calls at 2 am to find out if his requisition for a turret lathe operator has been filled and, if so, when the new person will report.

The center should also have broad authority to act (such authority to be defined by you) as is needed, even in derogation of another area's jurisdiction. You might, for instance, grant the center the power to hire new employees when Personnel is closed, pay new suppliers who make their deliveries at three in the morning and want their money, and order Security to drive a frightened employee home when Security feels it is a waste of time and manpower to do so.

The center demands a prime location (preferably overlooking the plant's front entrance) with plenty of room. For its 24-hour operation it will require a "permanent" staff of at least three hand-picked, talented, and tireless coordinators and three secretaries. Of course, the size of the staff can vary considerably depending on the volume of strike activity, but you should overstaff initially. Again, the center can draft employees from other departments for temporary duty or special assignments. You will likely spend considerable time in the center.

The strike control center is equipped with:

1. A large, wall-mounted map of the facility showing the location of everything of any significance; the map should cover the company premises from fence to fence and show all gates, interior roads or drives, and not only every building but each floor of each building. The map should be of such detail that any staffer would be able to direct a security guard by telephone from any post to any trouble spot accurately and by the quickest possible route.

2. Several telephones and extension numbers. No one calling strike control should ever get a busy signal. Three telephones and three numbers are a minimum.

3. A supply of all forms related to the strike response, such as incident reports, employment applications, purchase orders, requisitions, vouchers, and W4s. In other words, all those forms used in the daily conduct of your business during normal times should be readily available from strike control during these abnormal times.

4. A list of the names, office and home telephone numbers, home addresses, and job skills of every employee of the company.

5. An assorted collection of support items including two typewriters, a dictating machine, cameras (still and movie, with lots of film, flashbulbs, and lights for night shooting), binoculars, a tape recorder, two-way radios, spotlights, flashlights, adding machine, copying machine, television set, cots and bedding, city maps,

first aid supplies, blackboard and chalk, bulletin board, keys to company vehicles, keys to all locked areas, a supply of cash and receipts, coffee pot, hot plate and eating utensils, food and coffee, small refrigerator, telephone directory, table and chairs, desks, filing cabinets, copies of union contracts, and the other usual office accessories such as staplers, typing and scratch paper, paper clips, and tape.

6. A posted list giving a 24-hour telephone number (if possible) and a name for: key company personnel (all officers, all department heads, you, all assistants you have named, and each member of each strike committee), local police, FBI, railroad police, fire department, ambulance service(s), county and state law enforcement agencies, state governor and attorney general, state labor department, water, gas, electric, and telephone companies (including emergency service numbers), city council, city offices (sewer, trash removal, street repair, traffic, and street lighting), state employment commission, legal counsel (home and office), temporary housing (apartments, hotels, motels, boarding houses, Y's), wrecker services, all vendors, subcontractors, customers, industry associations, newspapers, radio and television stations, local and national union officials, and regional National Labor Relations Board office.

Responsibilities of the Strike Control Center

Strike Activity Log. The center will compile and maintain a chronological history of all strike activity from all available sources. The log should begin before the strike. (For instance, a written statement from a foreman who suspects some of his employees may be attempting a slowdown—who, when, how, etc. Or a pattern of unusually high absenteeism in a unit.) Once the strike begins, everything that happens should be logged. A few examples: Names or descriptions of all pickets, the times they arrive, who replaces them and when, the gate each pickets, the wording of picket signs, make and license numbers of cars the pickets arrive in, copies of handbills distributed, identification of delivery trucks honoring the picket lines, utility or plant equipment breakdowns or malfunctions, notes of telephone conversations with union officials, instances of the police being summoned and the results, copies of minutes of contract negotiations, "hate" letters written to customers or the company, complaints of harrassment from customers, vendors, and employees, affidavits of witnesses to picket line or other problems related to the strikers, incident reports, absenteeism each day by department, new hires for each open position, rumors and the action taken to squelch them, press releases issued by the company and the union, meetings with customers, daily production reports and product shipments, material deliveries, and so on....day by day, hour by hour. The log must be current at all times and readily available for review by legal counsel and the Emergency Operations Committee. To a large extent, the log can be formalized. See Exhibit 37.

Estimate of Cost of Strike. Someone from Accounting can probably best handle this. From the company standpoint, losses include such items as reduced profits, additional overtime costs, and expenses of supporting the strike response, such as legal fees, additional security, equipment rentals, etc. This accounting of costs is particularly important if you have strike insurance, and also in the event you are able to sue the union for damages (should the strike be an illegal one or one in violation of contract). The form presented in Exhibit 38 may be used to compile your strike costs.

Of course, there are some offsets, such as at least temporarily lower group hospitalization and other insurance premiums. A special account should be established and all strike-related costs charged to it.

You should also estimate the cost to the strikers of the walk-out; you might have reason to use it in a press release or in a letter to the strikers. From their viewpoint, the cost of the strike includes lost wages (including the increase you had offered) and the dollar value of unavailable fringes. Beyond that it is difficult to estimate, because you will likely never know how many cars were repossessed or how many strikers paid for hospital stays your group insurance would otherwise have covered.

Preparation of Press Releases. The local media will likely want to know the company's position regarding the strike, and you should be ready to express it. (The union will certainly not be reticent about giving statements to the press.) You can begin preparing these statements now, but because some sticky legal questions may be involved, have them reviewed by your legal counsel before their release.

As an example of an inference that must be avoided, you must be certain that your releases cannot be construed as an attempt to negotiate with the strikers individually in derogation of the union: "Surely the more intelligent of the strikers will recognize the insanity of the action forced on them by this so-called union, and they will return to work and earn more than they have ever earned before." Also, you do not want your releases to be interpreted as an effort to rouse the public against the strikers. This is because an announced adverse reaction to the strike by the mayor or church fathers could convert the strike from economic to unfair labor practice if it is found your press releases were meant to plant the seed for it. Exhibit 39 is a sample release.

Communications Center for the Plant. The center must solicit information as well as record and act upon what it receives. Its staff will check daily with each department to learn of all new developments and problems to be solved: from equipment malfunctions, suppliers who are reluctant to deliver, overnight damage to perimeter fencing, to even a shortage of clean sheets or toilet paper. Problems the center staff cannot resolve will, of course, be routed to the people who can take care of them, with appropriate follow-up by center personnel to ensure that they are handled.

The center must also be in the position to answer a wide variety of strike-related inquiries. If legal counsel calls to get the name of the police officer who investigated a picket line disturbance, the center should have it. If a foreman calls to find out if he will get the parts he needs tomorrow, the center should not only know where they are, but also who to contact to ensure their timely delivery.

A final communications function of the center concerns the peace of mind of employees and their families. Employees should know, and should in turn advise their families, that they can depend on the center to receive and transmit their messages any time, day or night. In the same vein, the center checks out and is in a position to verify or squelch rumors. If word spreads among employees, for example, that pickets stoned several cars as they were driven across the picket line, a foreman can quickly learn from the center whether or not there is any truth to it and if so what response the company has made.

Picket Line Observation. The center will insure that the picket line is continuously observed. The observers will be loaned from departments that can spare them. Ideally, the observers will know many of the strikers. Generally, one observer for each entrance should be adequate. He will record the obvious data—number and identification of pickets, signs carried, handbills distributed—and will immediately inform the center and security of any instances of mass picketing, rock throwing, obscene or threatening language directed at employees or security, and the like.

In addition to the picket line observation, a photographer should be available to record any instances of illegal picket line conduct. Where the camera equipment is stored depends on the available facilities. If you have a guard shack at each entrance, that should be an ideal place. In any event, it should be stored out of sight, because its visual presence might be construed as an attempt to intimidate strikers in the legal exercise of the right to picket. The persons assigned to operate the equipment need not be professionals; guards can do an adequate job after thirty minutes training. Remember, however, that peaceful picketing is not to be photographed—such action by an employer is almost always held to be an unfair labor practice.

Record Duplication. The center will duplicate certain files and records and ensure their safety at an offsite location. The documents to be copied are those which, if destroyed, you would sincerely regret not having duplicated. Certainly the daily log and its attachments are among them, as are many of the forms presented in the exhibits section of this manual. Others include the personnel lists you will compile, all documents relating to the hiring of striker replacements, the records you are keeping of costs directly resulting from the strike, payroll records from the start of the strike forward, and copies of contract negotiation minutes.

Communication with the "Outside World." During the strike, the center will maintain appropriate contacts with the public utilities, city, county and state agencies, and police and fire departments you met with prior to the strike, if for no other reason than to keep them informed of the status of the strike and thank them for their continuing interest. And by all means, praise them in writing each time they give you assistance. If at all possible, name the specific person who helped. The telephone company supervisor who makes his way through a rowdy picket line to repair a transformer is more prone to do it again if he receives a copy of the thank-you letter you sent to his boss.

Processing New Employees. If necessary, the center will assist Employment in processing job applicants and new hires. Thus, if applicants should arrive at a time when the employment office is closed, they should know (perhaps by a statement in the ad or a sign on Employment's door) to go to the center for an interview and possible referral to a supervisor. This means, of course, that center personnel will need to be basically familiar with the requirements of all open positions. Given copies of the job descriptions and a short training session by Personnel, they should be able to handle it with no problems.

New hires, by the way, should be made to feel welcome, by both office personnel and their new foreman. Your new hires will be entering not only a new job but a tense, abnormal environment. Unless you are careful to view the situation from their standpoint and to resist the temptation to process and assign them as you would a shipment of parts, they may become inclined to feel they are no more than a necessary but burdensome component of your effort to beat the strike. This is not conducive to either high productivity or permanency. If you seriously intend to hire permanent replacements, then treat these new hires like permanent employees.

A written work schedule indicating department, foreman, job assignment, work days, shift start and finish times, lunch period, and break times should be provided each new employee the same day he goes to work. In addition, the center (as well as Personnel) should be able to furnish new employees public transportation and parking information, a listing of available accommodations in different price ranges, and have the forms needed to enroll in your fringe benefit programs. Exhibit 40 is a basic new employee orientation form.

Employee Parking. The center should also have the authority, co-incident with the department that normally handles parking on the company lot, to issue temporary permits up to the maximum number you have authorized. This, again, is because a valid need to issue parking may occur when the normal channels are closed and you do not want to risk a new employee having his tires slashed just because no one was in the front office and he had to park on the street. The normal issuer of parking will, of course, be notified by the center of all permits it gives out.

Plant Tours. From the first day of the strike and until a sense of normalcy returns to the facility, center personnel will tour each struck department of the plant every day during each shift. As a valuable supplement, encourage your vice-presidents to accompany the center staff. The purpose of these visits is two-fold; first, to ensure that the strike response is alive and well—food, bedding, and the other creature comforts are in plentiful supply, security coverage is adequate and visible, etc.; second, so that foremen and employees will know you are interested and concerned and to give them the opportunity to ask questions about "what's going on." Interestingly, while these people who are seeing to it that the product gets out are likely the most important element of your strike operation, they are also likely to be the least informed. You should consider that alloting a portion of your center staff's time to visiting your production employees is time profitably spent. The presence of a vice-president occasionally will add to the morale-building effect of these tours.

Letters to Strikers. The center staff will write, have typed or duplicated, and prepare addressed envelopes for one or more letters to strikers (and their spouses) at their homes. Note: The purpose of such letters is to encourage the recipients to quit the strike and return to work. Thus, if you are working diligently to permanently replace the strikers, you will have little inclination to send out such letters.

If permanent replacement is not your goal and you launch into a letter-writing campaign, you may factually state in your letters the events that led to the strike, your opinion as to why the negotiations broke down, and the company's final offer to the union. You may state why you feel the striking employees should return to work, and you may ask them to do so. However, you must say nothing that could reasonably be construed as a threat ("If you do not return by next Monday, you will probably never be able to return.") or promise of benefit ("The sooner you return to work, the sooner the company can demonstrate its gratitude."). Further, you must say nothing that may be interpreted as an attempt by you to deal directly with the individual strikers and undermine the status of the union as the representative of the employees ("The union has led you down the primrose path. There's not a man among you who can't handle his relationship with the company ten times better than that union could ever hope to."). Exhibit 41 is a sample letter to strikers. Circumstances can vary; *any letter sent to strikers must be reviewed by counsel.*

Employee Flyer. The center will prepare in advance a one-page handout to be distributed to all working employees as soon as the walk out occurs. It should outline the events leading to the strike and the company's good faith efforts to avoid it. It should further assure the employees that the company will continue operations and has taken all necessary precautions to guarantee their safety. Equally important, it will inform employees that while picketing will likely occur and is generally legal, the pickets have no right to ask their names or in any way interfere with their access to company premises. It will also urge employees to immediately report to Security any incident of threats or other form of harrassment. Exhibit 42 is a sample.

A final word about your three special committees, Production, Production Support, and Strike Control. It is very important that you know that they are taking action to complete their strike preparations. Once you have assisted each committee determine the scope of its tasks, have each prepare a chart outlining its assignments and the targeted completion date for each. See Exhibits 43, 44, and 45. Assign each committee chairman the duty of ensuring that his committee's chart is completed and kept current. Completed and maintained, these charts will enable you and the committee members to easily keep track of each committee's progress.

The Second EOC Meeting—
A Final Checkout

It is now about a week since the first EOC meeting. You know much more than you did about what it takes to prepare for and win a strike, but the EOC does not. Take the time necessary to review in detail what the special committees have been doing. The EOC members will be interested to know, for instance, that you have met with the local police and utilities, that you have decided if you will or will not employ the services of an outside security firm, that you have leased an offsite warehouse, that new fencing will be constructed on the "south forty," and so on. The more you keep the EOC members in the know, and give them the chance to comment on what is being done, the greater the support you will have from them. And if an EOC member correctly points out an error you have made during the past hectic week, be willing to freely and gratefully acknowledge it, and then correct it.

Take the time also to express your appreciation for the enthusiasm and diligent efforts of the members of your special committees. They will appreciate hearing you praise them before their peers and superiors.

Take up the questionnaire that has been completed for each department since the first EOC meeting and announce that individual department strike plans based on these questionnaires will be distributed to each department head committee member at the third EOC meeting. (After this second EOC meeting, have the center staff extract useful information from them, such as employees who can be loaned to other areas and potential problems that can best be handled by one of the special committees. Also, have the center personnel prepare for each department a strike responsibilities outline. Each will include intradepartment duties, which are better performed within and by the particular department and are not likely to be crucial to the strike operation.)

Next, have your chief labor negotiator review the bargaining situation. The committee should be made aware of any changes in the stance of either party since the first meeting. Your negotiator should editorialize, too, and give the committee his predictions as to what he expects the union to do in the next several contract meetings. Allow ample time for the EOC members to question your negotiator following his talk.

Finally, go around the table and give each member the opportunity to make comments about the preparations being made in his department and to ask any questions he may have. (To get the ball rolling, it might be helpful if in advance of the meeting you think of a question or two to ask each member.)

Set the date and time for the third EOC meeting.

Are You Ready?

No, you are not ready, but you have begun and the hardest part is over. Hustle is now the name of the game. You will continue your EOC and special committee meetings, and schedule other meetings, projects, new committees, what-have-you, as you deem appropriate and necessary. Just remember, once you accomplish what has been outlined here, the rest—dealing with the strike—is easy.

"The Answers in the Back of the Book"

Actually, not *the* answers, but, it is hoped, thought-provoking questions and possible approaches toward answering them.

In the course of your strike preparations and certainly during the strike itself, you will take many actions in which you run the risk of transgressing a federal labor law. And, as stated when we began, there is no point in winning the strike on the picket line and losing it in court. Thus, this final exercise.

Call together the chairmen of your special committees, your chief labor negotiator, and your most valuable assistants for a lengthy brainstorming session.

Turn on your tape recorder and ask those present to think of any and everything that could go wrong from this point on and the proper response to salvage the situation. They should come up with at least a hundred ideas, the more the better. The questions are what are important for now. The answers can be found or improved upon later.

You will each come out of the session more confident and better equipped for the challenges ahead.

What follows is a "sampler" to help you get started. As you read it, bear in mind this last warning: The language of collective bargaining contracts and the infinite number of fact situations that may occur make it impossible for there to be many pat answers to labor law questions. The fact that the NLRB handles more cases each year than it did the year before is evidence enough that in the context of labor law two plus two is seldom four. Therefore, the "answer" given after each of the following questions is intended only to guide you in seeking an answer should you in fact have to respond to one of these questions "for real." This does not mean the answers are inaccurate; they are intended to represent the general rule. Just do not rely on them for more than they are.

1. *Two days after the walk-out a striker collapses at home with a heart attack. Is he covered under the group hospitalization insurance? If he dies a week later, is he covered under the group life policy?*

You already know that you as the employer are not required to help finance the strike, and it is highly unlikely that you are under any contractual or other obligation to continue paying group insurance premiums for strikers.

In the instant case, the answers may depend on what you have done before the strike and the policy language itself. Because the heart attack and death occured so soon, it is not unlikely that both premiums had been paid for the month in which the strike occurred. If that is the case, the striker probably has coverage until the time covered by the premiums runs out. But read the policy; it may provide that coverage can be cancelled upon written notice to the insurance company and that excess premium (including any paid by the striker) will be refunded. Act fast.

And read the labor agreement. Again, quite likely it will not require you to continue fringe benefit payments, but double-check it anyway. One example of a contract requiring continuation of payment of insurance premiums would be if the contract provided that all conditions would continue in effect during a wage re-opener, and that is when the union goes on strike.

In any case, unless either the policy or the labor contract precludes it, notify the carrier in writing that you will not be making any additional premium payments on behalf of the employees (strikers) you name in your letter. Federal law does not require you to notify the union or the strikers that you are taking this action, but some states have laws that do. Check this out.

As for an interim plan whereby the strikers themselves pay the full premium to the carrier, the law is simply not clear. In fact, the Labor Board and courts seem to have successfully avoided addressing the question. However, the proper inference may well be that if the union clearly and reasonably requests such an arrangement, you will need to come up with a substantial, legitimate business justification for telling the insurance company you will not agree to it. This seems a bit rough on you as the employer, because the claims of these people who may well never return can have an adverse effect on your experience and cause your rates to go up. And if the strikers are permanently replaced and the strike is never officially called off, how many years would they be allowed to feed off your low group rates? Lurking somewhere in these speculations may be the legitimate, substantial business justification you would need.

Just to make a point, here is a factual example of what can happen if you do permit group insurance coverage to continue. An employee was on strike and walking the picket line. He was receiving strike benefits from the union and also directed the distribution of these benefits to other strikers. While he was picketing he was assaulted and injured. Because the company had not cancelled his insurance coverages, his hospital and surgical expenses were paid. He returned to work after the strike but thereafter missed work due to the injuries he received while on the picket line. As there had been no break in his insurance coverage he successfully claimed and was awarded disability benefits for these absences.

Here are some more general thoughts regarding fringe benefits for strikers:

In determining benefit eligibility for strikers it is well settled that where a work requirement must be fulfilled before an employee can be eligible for a benefit, strike time need not be counted as work time.

The NLRB has noted certain distinctions in benefit eligibility that bear this out and of which you should be aware. To the extent that fringes, such as vacation days earned, are based on time worked, strike time is not time worked. On the other hand, where the length of the vacation that can be earned is based on seniority, strike time does not constitute a break in seniority. For example, assume a company requires that an employee must work 200 days during a calendar year in order to earn a full vacation and provides for pro rata vacation where less than 200 days are worked.

In addition, during the first four years of employment, a maximum of two weeks annual vacation can be earned; in the fifth and following years three weeks can be earned. An employee with two years' seniority goes on strike in July after having worked 75 days that year; he is reinstated in late November and works another 25 days prior to January 1. He has worked one-half of 200 days and would therefore be eligible to take only one week of vacation. Thus, where a benefit is based on work, strike time is not work time. However, the employee's strike time would be counted in determining when he would have five years' seniority and be eligible to earn three weeks' vacation. The distinction, then, is between benefits based on *work* and benefits based on *seniority*.

The Board has also addressed the question of "magic" eligibility dates and has held such dates cannot be used to deny strikers benefits already accrued. In the example above, assume first that the contract provided that in order to be credited with vacation the employee had to be on the active payroll on December 31 and assume second that the employee was not reinstated until January 10. The employee could not be denied; he would be eligible for pro rata vacation based on the 75 days he worked before he went on strike.

Holidays are usually an easier question to resolve because most contracts base eligibility on the employee working either the day before the holiday, the day after, or both. Because employees on strike work neither of these days, holiday pay can be denied. The key is the work requirement; if there is no work requirement but only a "continuous employment" requirement, it seems the strikers would have a good argument.

2. *On the day the strike is called, four employees represented by the striking union are on vacation and two others are scheduled to start vacation next week. What do you do?*

First, you have no doubt already paid the four who are on vacation; they are entitled to the vacation pay they have received, so forget it. Second, you probably can reschedule the vacations of the other two until after the strike, particularly if you reschedule the vacations of nonstrikers for good cause (such as to be able to continue your operations). Whether or not the strikers can demand immediate payment in lieu of vacation depends on the labor agreement, your past practice, and how you treat such requests from nonstriking employees. Of course, if by the rules vacation cannot be carried over from one vacation year to the next, and the strike goes that long, you will end up paying "in lieu of" anyway.

3. *Suppose you also find that on the day of the strike two employees represented by the union are out on paid sick leave. Can you cut off their sick pay?*

The Labor Board has held that a company may properly discontinue such payments where the employer reasonably concludes that the ill employees ratify and support the strike. In one case in which the company prevailed, the employer based his conclusion of strike support on the grounds the employees gave no indication they would not have struck, the strike was supported by virtually 100% of the employees in the unit, and the sick employees subsequently ratified the strike (in this case, by not protesting when their sick pay was terminated).

However, in a very recent decision, the Board changed its policy. It is now the Board's position that for an employer to justifiably stop paying disability benefits to employees unable to work at the time of the strike, the employer must show that "it has acquired information that indicates that the employee whose benefits are to be terminated has affirmatively acted to show public support for the strike." It is small consolation but the Board did say the employee's service on the picket line will suffice as evidence of such support.

This is obviously an unfortunate decision from the company's viewpoint. But, this decision underlines the importance of retaining counsel who will keep you current with the ebb and flow of labor decisions.

4. What is this "cooling off" period people are talking about?

Section 8. (d) of the Act provides that either party to a collective bargaining agreement seeking to modify or terminate it must give the other party 60 days notice and continue in effect the terms of the contract for that period or until the expiration of the agreement, whichever is later. Also, within 30 days of this notice, the Federal Mediation and Conciliation Service must be advised, if no settlement has been reached. With the exception of unfair labor practice strikes, walk-outs during the "cooling off" period are unprotected.

The same is true of a strike occurring within 30 days after notice to the FMCS, even if the party was late in notifying that agency. Thus, if the union gives the employer 60 days notice but does not notify FMCS until 40 days later, the "cooling off" period is 70 rather than 60 days.

5. Why don't we just save time and money and lockout the union employees?

A lockout may be a fine tactic, depending on your production situation and your bargaining goals, but consider it from all angles before you turn the key. And by all means, consult your counsel.

Originally, the Labor Board distinguished between "defensive" and "offensive" lockouts. The former, considered legal, was undertaken in order to avoid financial loss when the union was unwilling to give advance notice of a strike or other assurance of continued work. The "offensive" lockout, however, effected as a means of placing economic pressure on the union to agree to the employer's bargaining position, did not receive Board sanction.

Subsequent court decisions changed that, and today both types of lockouts may be legally instituted. However, there is still one major distinction in their permissible use. In a defensive lockout the employer may hire temporary replacements in order to continue operations. In an offensive lockout, hiring temporary replacements has been judicially condemned, although the Labor Board has condoned the employer's use of supervisors and nonunit employees to continue production.

6. *What is the employment status of a striker who is reinstated?*

Generally, the returning striker is entitled to reinstatement in his regular job without loss of seniority or other rights to which his seniority entitles him. He is not to be discriminated against in his status as an employee because he exercised his legal right to strike. Of course, this only applies to strikers who have a legal right to reinstatement, not persons who have engaged in illegal or unprotected strikes and have been discharged. These latter have no reinstatement rights and should you reemploy them, they can be treated as you would treat any new employee.

An unfair labor practice striker, of course, is really in the driver's seat when he applies to return to work. Unlike the economic striker, he is entitled to immediate reinstatement even if he has been replaced and you have to discharge or reassign his replacement in order to accommodate him. He is also entitled to back pay from the time he applies until he actually goes to work if it can be shown that the employer has unjustifiably delayed putting him back on the payroll. On top of that, the unfair labor practice striker is entitled to the full value of any fringe benefits he lost as a result of the strike. Thus, if he had to pay an uninsured $5000 hospital bill while he was on strike, and his group insurance would have paid it had he been at work, the employer must reimburse him. This should press home the importance of your strikers being economic strikers at the outset, and remaining economic strikers for the duration of the walkout.

7. *What rate of pay can be offered striker replacements?*

No more than was offered the strikers. It is an unfair labor practice to offer higher wages, more comprehensive benefits, or better working conditions to replacements than you offered those they are replacing. The Board will look very closely at a charge that you have transgressed this rule. It is not unlawful, however, to permit replacements to work many hours of overtime, even if overtime was virtually unheard of before the strike. And you are in no danger of being successfully charged with providing striker replacements with better working conditions if you find it necessary to furnish them beds and food during the strike. The law recognizes that you have the right to take certain steps to ensure that your operations continue. Freely authorizing at least plausibly necessary overtime and seeing to the safety and comfort (and maximum utilization) of your employees are among them. It is only when you begin to overdo it that the Board looks askance. Thus, while there is nothing wrong in continuing your normal promotion policy within the struck units, it might well be difficult to show legitimate business need to promote every new employee by four labor grades after his first week on the job.

8. *Almost all of our probationary employees went on strike with the rest of the unit employees. Do we have to put up with that?*

According to a court decision that addressed the question, it appears you do not. Under the terms of the labor agreement in that case, new hires were considered to be probationary employees for sixty days, and during this period they accrued no seniority and had no access to the contractual grievance procedure if the company terminated them. It was the employer's well established and adhered to policy to discharge any probationary employee who missed work during this sixty-day period. When the unit employees went on strike, the employer fired all the probationary employees. The union filed unfair labor practice charges. The court ruled in favor of the employer, on the basis that the probationary employees were terminated for absenteeism in accordance with the employer's standard practice and not because they had gone on strike. The court also stated that in resolving questions such as this, the employer's motivation is important and the court found the company had not acted out of antiunion animus.

Can you rely on this ruling? It seems questionable in some respects. For instance, suppose you had a long-standing, well-enforced plant rule that *any* employee who missed work five days in a row would be discharged. Could you use this rule to legally discharge every employee who went on strike? It hardly seems likely; the enforcement of such a rule would clearly destroy the right to strike as specifically provided for in the Act. Further, this result would occur not through negotiated agreement on the specific issue (as in a no-strike clause), but through a perhaps strained interpretation of a rule regarding absenteeism in general.

In a subsequent Board case, an employer terminated an employee who went on strike after being employed only one day. When a charge was filed, the employer argued that the decision was based on his policy of terminating new employees after three days of unreported absence. The Board found that the employer had good reason to know the employee had gone on strike and held the discharge to be unlawful.

There does not appear to be a significant distinction between the two cases. This is clearly a situation your counsel should review if and when it arises.

9. *A striker crosses the picket line and returns to work. Can he be fined by the union?*

Absolutely. And heavily. In fact, fines running into the thousands of dollars have been judicially enforced against union members.

However, the union cannot fine *nonunion* employees. Therefore, if the employee resigns from the union *before* he returns to work, his union cannot touch him.

The court decisions have left open the question of the extent to which a union constitution or by-laws can restrict the right of members to resign. In most, and perhaps all, cases, a written notice to the union of immediate resignation will protect the employee. The law is simply not clear on this important question.

Ideally, a striker desiring to return to work will ask you if he can be fined by his union if he does not first resign, and you can tell him. But if he does not ask, should you say anything? A qualified "yes." Inasmuch as you have not solicitated the striker's return, there could hardly be any wrong in your making a statement to the effect, "The union has the right to fine members who cross the picket line and return to work." But go no further; do not encourage the striker to resign. The decision must be his own.

In this same vein, suppose some strikers cross the line and return to work, and the union not only levies fines but sues your employees to collect them. Can you offer them any assistance? The Board has held that a company did not act unlawfully when it offered such employees

the services of the company's legal counsel at no charge. This was because the employees who returned to work did so based on their own
personal convictions and were in no way induced by the company. Of
course, if your returning employees did not first resign their union
membership, free legal counsel may be small consolation.

10. *What about supervisors? Can the union fine your foremen who,
even though they have not been in the bargaining unit since their pro-
motions, have retained their membership in the union?*

In the first place, you should not have foremen in this category. You
can legally instruct them to either resign from the union or give up their
supervisory positions.

The answer to the question is a qualified "yes." The law is now clear
that supervisors who are union members can be fined if they cross the
picket line and perform bargaining unit work. However, if they perform
only their usual supervisory duties during the strike, the union cannot
levy a penalty against them.

11. *You hire a permanent replacement with the understanding he
has to give his current employer a week's notice. Before he reports the
striker he is replacing applies for reinstatement. Do you have to take
the striker back?*

Probably not. So long as you can establish that there was a definite
commitment to hire the new employee on a permanent basis, you can
tell the striker his job has been filled.

12. *The strike center receives a call at 2:00 a.m. that a group of
about fifteen men is moving from the far end of the parking lot toward
the rear entrance to the plant. The guard who calls thinks some of them
are carrying pipes. What actions do the center personnel take?*

Because this is a hypothetical question at this point, it can be exam-
ined at some leisure. For one thing, how did they get in? Did you forget
about erecting entry-proof fencing around the perimeter of your facility? And how about lighting? If your lighting was enhanced as previously
recommended, surely one of your guards (you do have guards patrolling
the lot at all times, of course) would have seen them cutting through or
climbing over the fence. Strong, high fencing, bright lights, and grounds
area security would probably have dissuaded the strikers from making
this foray in the first place.

Too late for that now. So, first, while the staffer is still on the phone (or radio) with the guard, he instructs a co-staffer to call the police and tell them fifteen men are attacking at the rear of the plant, carrying weapons, and to request massive assistance immediately. Then he asks the guard how many minutes or seconds it will take the mob to reach the building. End of conversation.

The staffer then calls Security to tell them this (they may already know and probably should) while the co-staffer calls the supervisors of the work areas nearest the rear entrance to alert them and tell them that while neither they nor their employees are to risk getting into a brawl, they should move any portable, valuable equipment to a safe place.

Security makes an all-channel radio call to order all guards near the point of attack to assemble there at once. (But not the guards a considerable distance away, because another group might be waiting to see if the front entrance is left unsecured.) Security also has the designated individual take out the movie camera and lights and head for the scene of the action.

With any luck, the rear doors can be locked and a guard or two will be able to halt the strikers with words long enough for security personnel and, even better, the police to arrive. Now, while your security people can be expected to offer some spirited resistance to an attempt by the strikers to enter the plant, you should not expect them to be willing to die to keep the intruders out. The same is true for your other employees. Serious injuries to either side will not likely benefit your cause in the long run. Just try and be sure the violence by the strikers is filmed. That will be of more value in terms of criminal prosecutions than whatever equipment damage occurs before the police arrive and restore order.

The four main points, then: (a) make your property as secure as you can *before* anyone tries to break in; (b) be sure that the police are called *immediately*; (c) have a movie cameraman available at all times; and do not risk serious injury to your security people and other employees.

13. *An attack on the plant is not pleasant to think about, and engaging an outside security firm is sounding better all the time. How can you be sure you contract with the best one available?*

While firm A may have a better national reputation than firm B, within a given locale B may far excel A. Here are some items to check on each firm you contact:

•What strikes in your area has the firm worked lately? (Call these companies to get their appraisal of the firm's competence.)

•Does the firm include in its contract the services of a "strike captain" to oversee and coordinate your security operation?

•How many of the contract guards will be permanent employees of the firm and how many will be temporaries who have never been near a strike?

•How soon after you give the okay can the firm's guard force be on duty?

•What equipment will the firm furnish? Does it have vans available for transporting employees across picket lines? Will it provide its guards with radios?

•What is the reputation of this firm's guards with the police in cities in which the firm has worked strikes? Did they handle themselves professionally or were they boozers eager to knock heads with the pickets? Or, at the other extreme, did they end up looking the other way when the strikers became rowdy?

Overall, the firm's reputation in your area is probably the best indicator of its competence. If the firm you conclude is best qualified is also the most expensive, it is most likely well worth the additional cost.

14. *A truck of a common carrier is honoring the picket line and you need the materials.*

Call the carrier, explain the holdup, and demand delivery. Remind the carrier of its obligation under ICC regulations to make the delivery. Suggest that the carrier have a supervisor drive the truck across the line. If all else fails, be sure you have your own truck and driver available to pick up the load at your off-site delivery point.

15. *You have replaced 218 of 264 economic strikers. Through the union, the strikers offer to return to work provided all 264 are taken back. Are you obligated?*

No. The offer is conditional. You are not even required to reinstate 46 strikers based on this offer.

Let us take a closer look at offers to return to work. The Board and courts have made it clear they must be *unconditional* to be binding on the employer. Return-to-work offers can be made either by an individual striker or by the union on behalf of the striker(s).

The following applications for reinstatement were held to be conditional: a former full-time employee applies for part-time work only; an offer to return only if certain changes in work assignments are made; an offer by economic strikers to return only if their permanent replacements are discharged; an offer to return only if the employer agrees to resume bargaining with the union.

How do you distinguish between conditional and unconditional offers? Look for a requirement in the offer that you take some action *before* the striker will return. "I am unconditionally offering to return to work provided. . ." Take the time necessary to be sure it *is* conditional before you reject it. Back pay begins to accrue if you are wrong.

16. *If there is one good thing about the strike, it is that at least you do not have to keep negotiating, right?*

Probably wrong. In fact, if you had reached an impasse in bargaining (which does suspend the duty to bargain) before the union struck, the strike breaks the impasse and, upon the request of the union, you are back at the table again.

Some strikes do, however, give you a break from negotiations; such as strikes in violation of a valid no-strike provision of the labor agreement and slowdowns. So long as either of these two continues, you are relieved of the duty to bargain with the union.

17. *What is an impasse, anyway?*

An impasse occurs during bargaining when neither party is willing to make any further concessions on the issues. This can happen early or, if a skilled negotiator wants to avoid it, almost never. Once impasse on the issues occurs, and not before, the employer can unilaterally put into effect the wage and benefit increases (or other contract changes) proposed to and either agreed to or negotiated to impasse with the union. All strike replacements could legally be granted these proposed wage and benefit increases. (Effecting a *larger* wage increase or *different* contract change, however, would be an unfair labor practice.)

Impasse often immediately precedes a strike. Typically, the employer declares the impasse and puts into effect the proposals he has been over with the union; the union then calls a strike and files unfair labor practice charges alleging that the employer has been bargaining in bad faith from the very first negotiating session.

If the impasse is in fact a legal one, that is, if the employer has bargained in good faith with the intent to reach an agreement, then the company should be in good shape before the Board. (Note: Do not forget that even though you must bargain in good faith you are not by law required to agree to anything. The law demands good faith bargaining, not concessions, and expressly provides that the duty to bargain "does not compel either party to agree to a proposal or require the making of a concession."

Reaching a *legal* impasse is of paramount importance, because it is unfair labor practice, not economic, strikers who walk out following an impasse brought on by the employer bargaining in bad faith. And, as mentioned earlier, an unfair labor practice striker carries considerably more weight than an economic striker.

Although perhaps a bit beyond the scope of this manual, it could not hurt to discuss some ways to help ensure that if you reach an impasse it is a legal one.

Although as stated before, the law does not require you to have agreed to anything to prove you bargained in good faith, there is no doubt it is a big help if you can show you conceded to some of the union's demands.

Actually, this is not unreasonable, because in determining the merits of a bad faith bargaining charge, the Board is usually making a very subjective inquiry. You say you bargained in good faith, the union says you did not, and it is unlikely your honest face alone will sway the hearing officer. In resolving this dilemma, the Board and the courts look to other evidence surrounding the negotiations. The fact that you reached agreement on several issues prior to impasse does seem to indicate you were making an honest effort.

There are, however, certain bargaining positions that are per se illegal and support a charge of bargaining in bad faith. These include:

- •Refusal to bargain regarding a mandatory subject advanced by the union. Mandatory subjects are those that derive from the requirement of the Act that employers bargain concerning "wages, hours, and other conditions of employment." Some examples of mandatory subjects include bonuses, merit increases, incentive pay, holidays, insurance, vacations, shift hours, hours in the workweek, and plant rules. There are many more.

•Bargaining to the point of impasse regarding a "voluntary" subject. Voluntary subjects are just that. Either side may advance them but neither may condition execution of a contract on their acceptance. Some voluntary subjects are: the definition of the bargaining unit; a requirement that an employee must sign any grievance he files; union performance bonds; a requirement that the contract spell out the size and make-up of the union's grievance committee; that pending unfair labor practice charges be dropped; and who the parties to the contract are to be.

•Demanding that the other party bargain concerning an 'illegal' subject. An illegal subject cannot be included in the labor agreement even if both parties agree to it. Some examples are: that the company have the right to discharge an employee for union activity; that the union prove its majority status by secret ballot whenever the employer so demands; and that the union waive its right to be present at the first step of the grievance procedure.

Such per se violations generally are not present to make the decision of the Board an easy one. Instead, the Board normally must examine the "totality of conduct" of the employer in making its good or bad faith bargaining decision. Following are many of the factors the Board considers. As you read them, think about ways to ensure that you are on the good faith side of each in your negotiations.

•Is the employer available to meet at reasonable times and locations or does he continually delay or cancel meetings?

•Does the company representative have sufficient authority to represent the employer or is he strictly a messenger?

•Does the employer make any concessions or counterproposals or is his position fixed from the outset?

•Does the employer take inconsistent positions and frequently withdraw offers?

•Is there a stable bargaining history between the employer and the union?

•Has the employer successfully reached agreements with other unions?

•Does the employer honor the reasonable requests of the union for information relating to the issues?

•Are the employer demands such that the authority of the union would be decimated by their incorporation into the agreement?

•Did the employer adopt a "take it or leave it" attitude early in the negotiations?

•Did the employer make statements outside the negotiations that indicate he has no intention of reaching a settlement on the issues?

There are some other steps you can take to prepare for a hearing regarding your bargaining conduct. Be sure someone takes comprehensive minutes of each negotiating session. These minutes can support your position that you willingly discussed the issues, made verbal counterproposals, changed your position on issues (compromised), and made concessions. Also, your witnesses will find the minutes very helpful for refreshing their memory prior to testifying.

You should also prepare a summary of the negotiations in chart form. Your summary will show the date and duration of each meeting, the issues discussed (X), and agreements reached (A). For instance:

Date / Length		Wages	Ins.	Sick Pay	Holidays	(etc.)
6-4	2 hrs.	X	X	-	X	
6-6	2.5 hrs.	X	X	X	X	
6-7	2 hrs.	X	X	A	-	
6-8	4 hrs.	X	X	-	X	

One final word on this "beyond the scope of this manual" subject. As already mentioned, probably the most persuasive evidence of good faith bargaining you can advance is a lengthy list of resolved issues. Be sure you know which demands, yours and those of the union, are truly strike issues and which are not, and do not let pride prevent your reaching agreement on the latter.

18. *You decide to sue the union for lost profits during the first month of the strike. Can you?*

Probably not, unless the strike is an illegal one or is in violation of a valid no-strike clause of an existing contract. Economic strikes following impasse in bargaining are a legal weapon of labor. However, even in an economic strike, it may be possible to win an award for damages (in addition to an injunction) based on mass picketing and violence.

19. *The kitchen of the cafeteria burns. How will you feed the troops?*

Well, you have previously talked with several caterers about the possible need for some fast service, have you not? Or have you already worked out an emergency plan whereby food will be brought in for designated employees to prepare? (You can get by on sandwiches for a day or two if there is no other choice.) How soon can the damage be repaired? Can maintenance employees do it? If some food is undamaged in the fire, this might be a great time to call a break and give everyone a free meal.

20. *If for the first few weeks of the strike you can produce only one of your four products, which will it be and why? For which do you have the most orders in-house? For which product is it the least difficult to shift other workers to in terms of required skills, training, and the like? For which products do you have the most understanding customers? In what order and when will you phase in production of the other three?*

21. *You foresee that training will be needed for about 60 striker replacements in 4 job skills. How will you handle this?*

Ideally, prior to the strike you anticipated your training needs, at least in a general sense. In so doing, you located several available instructors, some perhaps from the ranks of your supervisors and others through contacts with local colleges or trade schools. Another possible source is the manufacturers of your production machinery. It will be expensive but you can probably arrange to have service reps come in and give your new employees concentrated courses in the operation of the equipment. Whatever the source, try to get commitments before the strike from each instructor, including the days of the week and hours each day he will be available, and for how long.

Your training courses should be a combination of classroom study and on-the-job training, heavy on the latter. Thus, you should provide for in-plant classrooms, with tables and reasonably comfortable chairs, blackboard, chalk, projector, screen, and so on. You should be able to get operator and repair manuals for your machinery from the manufacturer. These will certainly expedite the learning process, and you should have these on board before the walk-out. You also need to arrange for times during which your trainees can work on production itself, under the helpful eyes of the instructor and competent employees.

Also, because the employees who need training will not all be hired the same day, you need to be able to stagger your courses, with, say, a new class beginning each week for each of the 4 jobs. New hires will learn more quickly in small groups, but you may need more instructors than you first thought.

Do not forget—training time should be paid. If during a week a new employee is in class 10 hours and on the line another 40, that is 50 hours for which he is to be paid. Of course, if you utilize any nonexempt employees as instructors, the time each spends teaching, either in the classroom or on the job, is to be counted as worktime. That is also a good policy to implement for your exempt employees who instruct. The overtime you will pay thereby is money well spent.

22. *During the strike you discharge a striker for what you believe to be good cause based on picket line misconduct. He files an unfair labor practice charge and wins. Your only consolation is that you do not owe him any back pay unless he applies for reinstatement and you unlawfully delay or refuse his return to work. Right?*

Wrong. The Board has recently overturned a policy it had followed for 30 years by declaring in a 3-2 decision that back pay liability runs from the date of the illegal discharge. The best the employer can do once it is determined that the discharge was unlawful is rescind it and offer immediate reinstatement. If the striker refuses the offer, then it may be presumed he is still supporting the strike, and back pay liability will cease at that point. This is an unfortunate decision that may be overturned on appeal. In any case, it makes it especially imperative that you are careful to ensure that you have a strong case before you terminate any striker for misconduct.

23. *Okay, let us suppose some pickets are acting up. How can you be sure you have that strong case you need to justify their discharge?*

This is another of those questions that is often difficult to resolve. As one court stated: "The employee's right to engage in concerted activity may permit some leeway for impulsive behavior, which must be balanced against the employer's right to maintain order and respect."

However, case studies clearly indicate that the Board views misconduct much more leniently than the courts. This is unfortunate because you may properly discharge a picket but be forced to appeal an adverse Board decision in order to prevail. Here are some examples of such situations:

- A picket told some supervisors who were removing nails from the company's parking lot, "...there'll be two in your driveway at home for every one you pick up." The Board ordered the picket reinstated, but the court let the discharge stand.

- The same result obtained in the instance in which a picket told a nonstriker he would use a stick on her if she showed up for work again. The Board felt this presented no real harm or threat of harm; the court disagreed.

- Another picket told a nonstriker, "There are ways to keep you from going to work." The Board considered this an ambiguous threat and little more than picket line braggadocio. The court saw it differently.

- A picket hit a nonstriker's truck with a raw egg. Merely impulsive, exuberant behavior, said the Board. The court upheld the discharge.

- A picket asked a nonstriker if he thought his wife and children were safe. Not clearly a threat according to the Board, but the court held the discharge to be for good cause.

In summary, to legally discharge for misconduct at or away from the picket line, first be sure you can prove who did or said it. In the case of an act, look for intent to harm persons or property (or that the act itself evidenced a genuine potential for harm, such as brandishing a gun), and in the case of a statement, that the statement would reasonably be taken as a threat—"If you go inside that plant, you're a dead man."

24. *During the strike, six employees have a change of heart and return to work. For group insurance purposes they are treated as new hires and told they will have no coverage for 90 days. Is this safe?*

Of course not. The returning strikers are not new employees and to treat them as such has been held to be "inherently destructive" of the right to strike.

25. *An employee from Accounting honors the picket line out of sympathy for the strikers. Can you discharge him?*

No. But you can replace him. The general rule is that the employee is considered to have joined in the strikers' common cause and to have thus become a striker himself. Thus, you can treat him as you would any striker. The same rule applies if he crosses the picket line but refuses to accept a temporary transfer to perform struck work.

Suppose, however, another employee from Accounting refuses to cross the picket line out of fear for his personal safety. To what extent is he protected by the NLRA? Actually, the Act does not protect him at all. You can discharge him if you so choose. He is not refusing to cross the line out of sympathy for the strikers, and he therefore has no protected reason for not coming to work.

26. *Several employees represented by the maintenance union (not the union on strike) also honor the picket line. The maintenance contract has a no-strike clause. Can you discharge these employees or are you limited to replacing them?*

The answer depends on the precise wording of the no-strike clause and the grievance and arbitration language of the contract. If there is a clear waiver of the right to strike combined with an all-encompassing grievance/arbitration procedure, you may be able to make a discharge stick. But have the contract language reviewed by counsel in advance.

In one case, members of a clerical union refused to cross a picket line established by strikers represented by a production area union. The company discharged the clerical workers, based on the existence of a no-strike clause in their contract, and refused to reinstate them after they made an unconditional offer to return to work. It was subsequently determined that these employees should have been treated as economic strikers entitled to reinstatement because the no-strike clause did not preclude them from honoring the other union's picket line. The no-strike clause in that case prohibited strikes based on disputes and controversies "arising under or in connection with the terms or provisions" of the contract. The activity in question was held not to be encompassed by that language. The company would have had a stronger case had there been additional language prohibiting strikes arising from "differences regarding matters not specifically mentioned in this agreement" or even "any local trouble of any kind."

As a moderately interesting aside, you might want to consider the rights of striking versus discharged employees to unemployment compensation. In many states, employees on strike are as a matter of state policy not eligible for this benefit, even if they have been denied reinstatement because their jobs have been filled by permanent replacements. On the other hand, employees discharged for good cause are generally eligible to collect benefits after a "penalty" period, which may be as short as one week. Conceivably, then, you might want to replace rather than discharge that frightened Accounting employee mentioned above. His inability to draw unemployment compensation just might give him the courage he needs to come on back to work.

27. *A picket is accidently hit by the car of a company official. Is he entitled to workers' compensation benefits?*

It seems unlikely; he is hardly acting within the course and scope of his employment.

28. *Just how familiar are you with the labor market in your locale? Do you know where to find the people with the skills you will need or for that matter where to find people at all? Assume you will be facing a tight labor market; can you name twenty sources of either temporary or permanent help? Consider the following:*

•Trade schools

•Part-time college students

•Community organizations

•Temporary agencies (labor contractors)

•"Position wanted" ads

•Billboards

•Employees on lay off from other companies

•Help wanted ads in newspapers

•Children of nonstriking employees

•Employment agencies

•Employees loaned from other companies

•Large sign in front of plant listing open jobs

•Announcements on radio and television

•Ads on bulletin boards in bowling alleys, washaterias, churches, etc.

•Handbills on cars in shopping center lots

•Employees retired from your company

•Referrals by your employees

•Your files of previously rejected applicants

•Referral of applicants by friends at other companies

That is nineteen; no one said it would be easy.

29. *An economic striker desires to return to work; he has not been replaced. He is told he will be reinstated only if he promises never to go on strike again. That is reasonable, is it not?*

It is not. If he unconditionally offers to return, that is the basis on which you must reinstate him—unconditionally.

30. *You send a letter to the striking employees in which you state ". . .no action will be taken against you if you desire to return to work." Is this a threat against those who do not want to return to work?*

Such a statement was held not to violate the Act because there was found to be no indication that any adverse action would be taken against those who did not return. The employer was simply attempting to assure the strikers who wanted to return that they would not be punished for what they had done.

31. *The strike occurs following an impasse that you declare. Because you declared it, then it is up to you to notify the union of your willingness to resume bargaining. Right?*

No. An impasse is an impasse. Where a strike follows an impasse it is the union that must initiate the resumption of bargaining. You can sit back and hope they do not call.

32. *In the course of negotiations during the strike, you reduce your pre-strike wage offer by half and propose eliminating all holidays and vacations. This is a good way to show them how tough you are, right?*

Could be, but find a better way. If you employ such tactics, you may well be successfully accused of *surface bargaining* (an illegal form of bargaining characterized by indications that the employer is merely going through the motions of negotiating), the result of which may be that the strike is suddenly converted from economic to unfair labor practice. You can bargain in good faith and be tough at the same time.

33. *During the strike a porter each week works 16 hours at his regular job and 32 hours on a struck job. His usual hourly rate is $3.50; the hourly rate for the struck job is $4.60. How do you compute his overtime?*

One way is to base his overtime pay on his average straight-time rate. Assume the work week is Monday through Sunday. He works Monday and Tuesday at his regular job (16 hours at $3.50 = $56.00) and Wednesday through Friday at the straight-time production rate (24 hours at $4.60 = $110.40). At straight-time, then, he earns $166.40, so his average straight-time rate is $4.16 ($166.40 divided by 40). Thus, his overtime rate if he works Saturday is $6.24 ($4.16 times 1.5).

Another way is to pay the employee at the overtime rate of the job that he is performing after he has worked forty straight-time hours. This arrangement requires the advance agreement of the employee. Applying this procedure to the above example, the employee's overtime rate for Saturday would be $6.90 ($4.60 times 1.5) if he does production work and $5.25 ($3.50 times 1.5) if he is working his regular job during overtime hours.

Be aware, however, of the provisions of the contract (whether or not it is expired) regarding overtime pay. This is because these provisions remain in effect where the contract has not been terminated and very likely still prevail after the contract expires except as to provisions over which you have bargained to impasse. Therefore, if the contract language calls for double time on Saturday regardless of the number of hours previously worked during the week, then check with counsel before you pay a lesser amount.

Even more complex problems arise in the case of exempt employees performing nonexempt bargaining unit work. Under the law, the exempt/nonexempt status of each employee is determined on a week-to-week basis. Thus, a systems analyst who during the strike spends most of his time oiling machinery is no longer an exempt employee; he is due overtime pay for weeks in which he works in excess of 40 hours. (You can, by the way, pay him his regular salary during this time and base his overtime on his salary converted to an hourly figure. In other words, he need not take a pay cut during the time he is performing other than his normal job in order to help you get the work out.)

You and your counsel must be familiar with the wage and hour regulations on this subject.

34. *How will you recognize mass picketing if you see it?*

That may depend on the laws of the state in which your plant is located. All states have statutes regulating picketing, and these laws generally provide for injunctions and criminal sanctions against picketing that unreasonably interferes with the conduct of a business or through coercion, intimidation, or deed endangers or threatens to endanger employee or public safety.

However, the laws of some states so broadly limit the right to picket that federal and state courts have condemned their literal application, either on the basis of unlawful interference with the First Amendment guarantee of free speech or infringement on the paramount jurisdiction of the National Labor Relations Act to regulate labor disputes.

In examining these state regulatory statutes the courts have attempted to balance the thrust of the First Amendment and the NLRA with the duty and authority of the states to preserve, as it were, the domestic tranquility. From the cases it appears the courts will often find the authors or enforcers of these state laws to have been overzealous.

As an example, the law of one state, among other provisions relating to picketing, limits pickets to not more than two within fifty feet of each entrance to the employer's premises. Recently, a state appellate court was called upon to review a temporary injunction issued by a lower court based on alleged violations of this law.

The facts of the case indicated that soon after a strike was called, some fifteen pickets parked their cars along the curb in front of the employer's building and scattered themselves up and down the street. They lounged on their cars and stood around talking in small groups. Three strikers confronted three new employees proceeding across the street toward the building entrance, but stepped aside when requested to do so by a member of management. Several witnesses testified the presence of the pickets frightened them. The appellate court dismissed the injunction because it found no evidence of either conduct marked by violence or imminent threats to the public order or of denial of access to and from the struck premises. Thus, the "mere presence" of fifteen or more pickets at or near the entrance to the employer's premises was not enjoinable under the state law.

One might well conclude from this decision that many state laws regulating picketing may not be strictly enforceable. Rather, it would seem to be more prudent not to seek injunctive relief until the pickets actually block a plant entrance with the clear intent to deny access to the premises; physically harm or threaten to harm employees or customers or the property of either; or engage in conduct closely approximating one or both the above. If you see one or more of these events taking place, you are likely witnessing illegal mass picketing, and it is time to get out the cameras and call your counsel.

Bear in mind, of course, that a picket can commit an individual act, such as throwing rocks at nonstrikers, that will subject him to valid discharge or criminal prosecution without regard to whether or not mass picketing is occurring at the time.

35. *How true is it that pickets must stay off private property?*

It is substantially true; pickets generally run the risk of being successfully charged with trespass if they enter private property without the permission of the owner.

There are, of course, exceptions. The exceptions come into play when the employer's property is isolated from a public thoroughfare. In such cases the pickets may be permitted to patrol on private property, the theory being that to limit picketing to the public property nearest the employer's location would likely enmesh employees of other employers in the dispute. Another exception has been carved out in the case of businesses located within shopping centers. Picketing is sometimes permitted within the boundaries of a shopping center on the basis that the strikers cannot be denied access to property that is generally open to the public. This (like many others) is a changing area of strike labor law; if you feel your situation might be subject to one of these exceptions, have your counsel review it for you.

36. *So many employees of your suppliers are honoring the picket line, you decide to bring in some Tennessee mountain men to clear the streets.*

That is a bad idea. It is a violation of federal law to transport any person across state lines if that person is to be employed to interfere by force or threat with peaceful picketing.

On the other hand, you are free to employ as strike replacements persons from out of state. One warning, however: Some states have enacted laws regulating the employment of these so-called "professional" strike replacements. One such law defines professional strike replacement as any person who has been employed anywhere two or more times in the same craft or industry in the place of a striking employee. The law goes on to provide (a) that no person shall recruit any professional strikebreaker to replace a striking employee in any company in which the person is not directly interested, and (b) that no professional strikebreaker shall take the place in employment of an employee on strike.

37. *There has been no strike as yet, but a lot of employees are talking about it among themselves, and a few are handing out leaflets in the parking lot. You can put a stop to this, right?*

The answer depends on your rule regarding solicitation and distribution and how you have enforced it in the past. The law now seems to be that you can forbid solicitation during actual work time (as opposed to the working hours) anywhere in the plant, and you can prohibit the distribution of literature in work areas during working and nonworking time. (Lunch periods and breaks are not work time though they are included in the working hours.)

Additionally, even if you have a valid rule on the books, unless you have consistently enforced it in the past as to all solicitation and distribution, you will not be able to begin enforcing it now.

38. *A couple of employees get so angry over the progress of negotiations they turn in their tools, demand their checks, and storm out in a huff. Later, after the strike begins, you see them walking the picket line. Still later, they unconditionally request reinstatement. Are they entitled?*

Probably not; the evidence indicates they resigned. Employees who quit are not on strike, and you can treat their applications as you would those of any applicants seeking employment.

39. *The strike has been in effect for almost a year. All the strikers have long since been permanently replaced. There is only an occasional*

instance of picketing, and the last time you had contract negotiations was a couple of months ago. Next time the union calls, can you refuse to meet on the basis the union no longer represents a majority of your employees?

That is a good question but not an easy one to answer in most cases. First, if it has been less than twelve months since the union was certified as the representative of the striking employees, a legal presumption exists that the union still represents a majority of the employees in the unit. So, yes, meet with the union.

In cases in which it has been more than one year since certification, the usual position of the Board is that the same percent of striker replacements supports the union as was the case before the strike. However, this presumption may not be applicable where almost all the unit employees went on strike and virtually all were replaced. If that is your situation you may be able to demonstrate to the Board that you have legitimate doubts concerning the majority status of the union. (Your opportunity to so demonstrate comes, of course, after you have refused to meet and the union has filed a refusal to bargain charge. Arguably you do not have much to lose should the Board order you to resume negotiations; it is not likely an adverse decision would convert the strike from economic to unfair labor practice, the strike having continued for so long, and there being no true causal connection between the charge and the original reason for the strike.)

However, you may prudently not want to risk a charge based on your refusing to resume bargaining. In that case, you may be able to file for a representation election (assuming again that it has been more than one year since the union was certified). To obtain such an election you must be able to show by "objective considerations" that you have reasonable grounds to believe the union no longer holds majority status. There are virtually no cases addressing this question, however, and it is difficult to state with any certainty what qualifies as an objective consideration.

Fortunately, an employee can file for and more easily obtain a decertification election. The employee need only show that at least 30% of the employees in the unit support the election request. (Again, the election can not be sought until at least twelve months have passed since the union was certified.) Employee support is usually demonstrated by employee signatures on a petition asking for the election. Of course, supervisors cannot file decertification election petitions, and such petitions *must not* be company inspired.

The persons eligible to vote include the permanent replacements, but not new employees hired on a temporary basis or current employees on temporary loan from other departments. The strikers are also eligible to vote if the election is held within twelve months of the start of the strike. (Do not confuse the certification and start-of-strike twelve month periods.) In some cases, certain strikers are not eligible to vote in any case; this is true for strikers whose jobs have been eliminated for valid business and economic considerations and strikers who have been legally discharged for misconduct.

40. *Come to think of it, is there any chance that the union is also making preparations for the strike?*

Unquestionably. Unions have strike manuals, too. What follows are some comments and recommendations from such a manual. You will find some interesting parallels.

> A strike is a war. The strike is a form of economic war. To fight a war is hell—to lose one keeps you in hell. So when a strike starts, the idea is to win. As in military war, preparedness is important in the strike war. That is the keynote of this manual. Be prepared! Do plenty of strike preparation work before the plant comes down and you will find fewer emergencies arising in the third, sixth, ninth, or twentieth week of the strike. Read this book long before you strike. Study it carefully if you think there is the remotest chance you may strike. The advice given in every chapter is best used *before the strike*.
> The strike is war. It is a last resort. Successful unionism is not best served by useless striking. Victory without a strike is always best. But the threat of a strike is often used as a weapon to obtain union demands.

The union recognizes three phases of the strike period. First, the initial two or three weeks of the strike will be relatively easy; most members will be in high spirits, some will be over-confident. The strike looks easy. However, after this initial period, morale will likely drop; the men miss a paycheck, and the novelty of the undertaking wears off. Some of the men will tire of strike work while others become bored from strike idleness. And third, if the strike is long, morale rebounds as the men realize there is no hope for a quick settlement. They doggedly resign themselves to the long grind.

The union survives the second period through the use of morale builders such as speeches by prominent labor leaders, Saturday night dances, movies, parties, card games, and the like. The resolve to get through the third period is bolstered by welfare and work committees and the continued use of morale builders.

Prior to the strike the membership must be conditioned. It is considered imperative that each member feels he has a personal stake in the action. The men must be convinced that they are right and the company is wrong.

The strike vote is considered to be of great importance. All the issues are to be voted on by the entire membership. Thus, none of the members can say later, "we never voted on that point," and thereby adversely affect morale.

It is also recommended that the community be conditioned to support the union position.

> If the public is supporting the strikers, judges will be less likely to issue injunctions, policemen will be less likely to make arrests. Even the company will be less likely to take unreasonable positions, for the company must maintain good will in the community in which it operates and sells its goods.

According to the union leaders, the community can be informed through newspaper ads, radio programs, leaflets, personal contacts (especially with merchants, ministers, and professional people), newspaper releases (to be given to the local editor before the strike), and contacts with peace officers and other public officials. The reason for the latter is to convince these officials that the union is trying to cooperate; this is supposed to make them feel good because each thinks he has a tough job and gets no understanding from the public.

Also, the wives are to be put to work on the basis that women work harder than men. Their participation will boost morale, and they will contribute skills the men do not have. The wives can work in the strike kitchen, solicit contributions, make door-to-door public relations contacts, distribute leaflets, address envelopes, and speak to women's clubs and church groups.

The formation of a strong strike organization is stressed. The Executive Strike Committee heads up the entire effort. Some of the other recommended committees are:

Picket Major. He is the leader of a group of picket captains, a desk sergeant, squadron leaders, a motor squadron, and strike police whose responsibility is to see that the picket lines are fully manned and that no one does less than his share of sign carrying.

Publicity. The job of this group is to prepare strike bulletins and news releases, write speeches, and provide general information to the public. Working closely with this committee are the *Interunion Liaison Committee* (Speakers Bureau) and the *Citizens Committee* (to maintain contack with influential people and administrative officials in the community).

Office of Records. This group handles picket schedules and related records, eligibility of strikers for public relief, receipts for contributions received, and records of fines levied.

There are also *work captains* who scour the area for employment opportunities for striking members; a *Solicitation Committee* which is responsible for obtaining donations of money and food; *Interviewers*, who screen the applications of strikers in need of money; a *Kitchen - Canteen* group; a committee of *Sergeants-at-Arms* to maintain order in the hall; and an *Entertainment* committee.

Good public relations are valuable:

> First reaction by the average citizen to a strike is likely to be one of disapproval. A strike causes trouble and he is against trouble. He figures the strike is the union's fault, because the union calls the strike. Our job is to convince the average citizen that the union was justified in striking, that no red-blooded men could have done less. We must convince him that he will profit if the workmen win more than if the profit-gobbling company wins.

Also, a research sub-committee is recommended. The material it gathers can be used to convince the public the company is taking an unfair position. The stated responsibilities of this group include:

•Examining the background of company officials. What companies have they worked for previously? What was their labor record in other plants? What were their favorite strike-breaking tactics?

• Determining past connections of company officials. Have they been connected with fascist organizations? (!) Do they have bloody records of labor fighting? If either is true, then the committee must let the public know.

• Examining the connections of the company with other companies. What companies will help the struck company by filling orders, etc.?

• Finding out if some company officials are paternalistic in nature. Any who are may be persuaded to temper the attitude of an unreasonable management. Letters can be written to them pointing out the attitude of the workers and their resentment against the anti-labor posture of the company.

Financing of the strike is given considerable attention. Strikers require money and the union reminds members that the eve of a strike is not an auspicious time to buy a new car on the installment plan.

How to collect money is discussed. As soon as the strike begins, members visit every local union in the area seeking not only lump sum contributions to but also pledges for weekly contributions. On paydays strikers can go the gates of unstruck plants and make collections. And certainly strikers who find outside jobs are expected to contribute a fixed percentage of their earnings to the cause. The manual suggests a close check be kept of these employed members; if someone misses a payment, locate him and collect it. Contributions of food are also important. Merchants should be told that the union members are the backbone of their businesses and that the union will make known their contributions far and wide.

The subject of welfare is given considerable play in the union strike manual. Members are not to expect miracles; payments must be small because the union's defense fund is limited. The entire community is to be mobilized behind the strike. Possible sources of outside public help are listed: unemployment compensation; child welfare service; aid to dependent children; county welfare departments; aid to blind; aid to crippled; vocational rehabilitation; Old Age and Survivors' Insurance (Social Security); public health departments; visiting nurses. Private welfare agencies are also recommended as potential sources of assistance.

Counteracting company propaganda is also stressed. It is suggested that the company will pull certain "tricks" to break the strike, each of which must be anticipated in advance:

•Letter writing is stated to be a favorite device of the company. The experienced striker will alert the other strikers that they will be receiving letters threatening them with loss of seniority and retirement benefits, the plant shutting down and moving to another locality, recitals of wages lost because of the strike, and other comments of that ilk.

•Company stooges will be everywhere, busily engaged in undermining morale.

•Rumors will be instigated by the company, most likely through stooges and foremen.

It is also recommended that arrangements be made in advance of the strike to have bail bonds available for emergency cases. A local attorney should be contacted for the purpose of ensuring help is available at all times to handle any arrests that may occur. The police, incidentally, are to be asked not to patrol the picket line simply because a strike is being called.

Certain pre-strike methods for bringing pressure on the company are mentioned. The Federal Mediation and Conciliation Service should be asked to assign a commissioner to meet with the parties; friendly state officials should be asked to call a joint conference of the parties or set up a public fact-finding committee to investigate the issues and make recommendations; the mayor might also be asked to do the above; ministers might be prevailed upon to attend meetings to which both parties are invited to discuss the issues; a company highly dependent on the to-be-struck company may be persuaded to intercede; a friendly stockholder of the company who does not agree with current management policy might be willing to intervene; and offering to arbitrate may have good public relations value because if the company refuses the community will get the feeling the union is trying to avoid trouble while the company is not.

A war of nerves regarding the strike date is recommended. During negotiations the strike vote should be mentioned frequently but nothing should be said that would indicate the specific date or hour of the walk-out. The company's fear of the impending strike may cause it to keep foremen on the job for endless hours. Also, if the company knows when the strike is coming, it can make arrangements that may enable operations to continue.

Interestingly, virtually no such tactics are outlined for use *during* the strike. Only one, "installment strike," is mentioned. Under the installment strike, the strikers offer to return to work shortly after the walk-out and before the company has had time to replace them. They may do this several times, thereby, in theory at least, keeping the company in turmoil.

The manual concludes with the assurance that no strike is ever really lost; that even if the strikers return to worse conditions than they left, they have gained something in showing the company their ability to strike.)

And *this* discussion concludes with the question what sort of victory would it be if the strikers *never* return?

Afterword

You may feel at this point that preparing for a strike is hopelessly complicated. It is true there is a great deal of work involved, but once you begin, the preparations are neither hopeless nor complicated. In fact, you and your committees will find it an exhilarating experience.

"Overdo" your preparations initially. Over-staff, over-order, over-stock, over-do. Later, if you have in fact over-done it, the situation will be easier to correct than if you had taken the opposite approach.

You likely will not complete every task or answer every question posed in this manual. Do not worry. If you give the preparations your best effort, it will be sufficient. If you do fail it will be simply because you never started. So start! Your strike response operation will soon develop a momentum of its own, and about the time of your third EOC meeting all the pieces will begin falling into place.

One more word about unfair labor practices. It appears from the cases that many companies found guilty have taken these unlawful actions out of ignorance of the law or plain and simple desperation. If you have competent counsel, prepare well, and look before you leap, there is no reason you cannot avoid the unfair labor practice pitfall.

From this point on, you are in charge. You probably will not need it, but . . . . good luck!

Forms, Memos, and Letters

Exhibit 1

(Assignment of Emergency Operations Manager)

CONFIDENTIAL

TO: ALL VICE - PRESIDENTS AND DEPARTMENT HEADS

Bargaining with _____ union has not progressed as well as I had hoped it would. Although I believe these current negotiations will be brought to a conclusion satisfactory to both parties, I feel certain action on my part is indicated at this time.

I have therefore given _____ the responsibility to address certain questions which may arise in the event these negotiations do not result in agreement.

Although his assignment concerns a situation which we all hope will not occur, it is imperative that he receive your usual full cooperation and support.

His assignment as Emergency Operations Manager is effective immediately.

Sincerely,

_____
CEO

Exhibit 2

(Announcement of First EOC Meeting)

CONFIDENTIAL

TO:

The Emergency Operations Committee will meet on _____,
_____, at _____ AM.

The responsibilities of the Committee will be outlined
and certain additional committee assignments will be announced.

Mr. _____ will review the present status of contract
negotiations with _____ union.

Your attendance and active participation are very important to the successful completion of the work of the
Committee.

If you will be unable to attend, notify me immediately
at extension _____ and let me know who will attend as your
alternate.

Sincerely,

_____
Emergency Operations Manager

Exhibit 3

(Questionnaire to EOC Members)

(Cover Letter)

(Date of first EOC meeting)

A strike by employees represented by _____ union now appears to be a real possibility. It is the intent of management to continue operations regardless of what action may be taken by this union.

Each department must be prepared to contribute, in regard to its own functions and as an integral part of the overall strike response.

Please complete the attached and return it to me at the next meeting of the Emergency Operations Committee.

Not all questions are applicable to every department.

If your answer to a question indicates that action is needed, indicate the steps being taken.

Emergency Operations Manager

Exhibit 3 (continued)

                                              Prepared by
                                              _____

                                              Date prepared
                                              _____

Department _____

Department Head _____   Extension _____

                                              Home phone _____

Assistant _____   Extension _____

                                              Home phone _____

EOC Alternate _____   Extension _____

                                              Home phone _____

Questionnaire answered by _____   Extension _____

                                              Home phone _____

1. Functions which cannot be suspended during a strike:

_____

_____

_____

2. Functions which can be suspended during a strike:

_____

_____

_____

_____

_____

_____

_____

Exhibit 3 (continued)

3. Will additional personnel be needed to maintain department functions? _____ If so, how many and with what
   skills? _____ _____

   _____ _____

   _____ _____

4. If the additional personnel will require training, of
   what type and duration? _____

   _____

   Who will the instructor(s) be and where will the training take place? _____

5. Are the alternate skills of department employees known
   and recorded? Where? _____

6. Are the home telephone numbers of department employees
   listed? Where? _____

7. Attach a list of the names and skills of department employees who can be loaned to assist other departments.

8. Can material be stockpiled? Where? _____

9. Can the department itself insure that essential deliveries will be received? How? _____

10. How can department material, supplies, and equipment be
    protected from sabotage? _____

    _____

11. How will the department operate if any of the following
    services are disrupted?

Exhibit 3 (continued)

Telephone _____

_____

Gas _____

_____

Electricity _____

_____

Water _____

_____

12. Have all suppliers been notified of the anticipated strike? _____

13. Have all customers been notified of the anticipated strike? _____

14. What, if any, of the department's work can be subcontracted, and to whom? _____

_____

Exhibit 4

VENDOR NOTIFICATION

Prepared by _____

Date prepared _____

Vendor _____

Notified by _____

Date notified _____

Person contacted _____

Title _____

Address _____

Telephone _____

Emergency telephone _____

Delivery or other problems anticipated: _____

_____

Describe additional costs which may occur: _____

_____

_____

Were Interstate Commerce Commission regulations discussed?

_____

Date scheduled for follow-up contact: _____

Exhibit 5

OFFSITE MATERIAL DELIVERY LOCATIONS

Prepared by _____

Date prepared _____

Name of facility _____

Owned by _____

Owner's telephone number _____

Address of facility _____

Distance from plant _____

Lease requirement _____

Cost _____

How soon available? _____

Disadvantages of facility _____

_____

Does railroad serve facility? _____

Is day labor available? _____

Is unloading equipment available? _____

Is facility used by other companies? _____

_____

Labor/union problems anticipated at this facility _____

_____

Exhibit 6

MATERIAL STOCKPILING CONSIDERATIONS

Prepared by
_____

Date prepared
_____

Material _____ _____ _____ _____

Days' supply on
hand this date _____ _____ _____ _____

Days' supply now
available for
delivery _____ _____ _____ _____

For how many days'
supply is storage
area available? _____ _____ _____ _____

Is offsite storage
area available? _____ _____ _____ _____

Material   Recommendation

_____   _____

_____   _____

_____   _____

_____   _____

Exhibit 7

OFFSITE WAREHOUSE LOCATIONS

Prepared by _____

Date prepared _____

Name of facility _____

Owner _____

Owner's telephone number _____

Address of facility _____

Distance from plant _____

Lease requirement _____

Cost _____

How soon available? _____

Square footage available _____

Does facility have own security? _____

Can facility be used as delivery location? _____

Is facility used by other companies? _____

_____

Does this facility meet our special storage requirements?

_____

_____

Does facility provide loading/unloading personnel? _____

Are facility personnel union? _____

Exhibit 8

MATERIAL STATUS SUMMARY

Prepared by _____

Date prepared _____

Based on an analysis as of __(date)__ :

1. No supply problems presently exist for the following:

   Material   Days' Supply Available

   _____   _____

   _____   _____

   _____   _____

   _____   _____

2. Arrangements will be made to pick up the following offsite:

   Material   Location

   _____   _____

   _____   _____

   _____   _____

   _____   _____

   _____   _____

3. The following will be stockpiled:

   Material   Location   Days' Supply

   _____   _____   _____

   _____   _____   _____

   _____   _____   _____

   _____   _____   _____

Exhibit 8 (continued)

4. Supply problems exist for the following:

Material	Problem	Solution
_____	_____	_____
_____	_____	_____
_____	_____	_____

5. As of this date Production would face no material short-ages for _____ days.

6. After resolution of material supply problems, Production would have on hand material as follows:

Material	% of normal needs	Number of days
_____	_____	_____
_____	_____	_____
_____	_____	_____
_____	_____	_____
_____	_____	_____
_____	_____	_____

Exhibit 9

ACCELERATED MAINTENANCE SCHEDULE

Prepared by _____

Date prepared _____

Equipment   Maintenance Needed   Assigned To   Complete By

_____   _____   _____   _____

_____   _____   _____   _____

_____   _____   _____   _____

_____   _____   _____   _____

_____   _____   _____   _____

_____   _____   _____   _____

_____   _____   _____   _____

_____   _____   _____   _____

Exhibit 10

EQUIPMENT STORAGE

Prepared by _____

Date prepared _____

Equipment/Machinery	Storage Location	Security Provided?
_____	_____	_____
_____	_____	_____
_____	_____	_____
_____	_____	_____
_____	_____	_____
_____	_____	_____
_____	_____	_____
_____	_____	_____

Exhibit 11

EQUIPMENT/MACHINERY SECURITY

Prepared by

Date prepared

Equipment/Machinery	Guard Needed?	How is area secured?

Exhibit 12

EXPEDITED PRE-STRIKE SHIPMENTS

Prepared by
_____

Date prepared
_____

Customer _____

Person contacted _____

Title _____

Telephone number _____

Date contacted _____

Normal delivery schedule:

Date	Product/Quantity	Shipper
_____	_____	_____
_____	_____	_____
_____	_____	_____

Customer will accept additional shipments as follows:

Date	Product/Quantity	Shipper
_____	_____	_____
_____	_____	_____
_____	_____	_____

Exhibit 13

SHIPPER NOTIFICATION

Prepared by _____

Date prepared _____

Shipper _____

Person contacted _____

Title _____

Telephone Number _____

Date contacted _____

Anticipated shipping problems: _____

_____

_____

Solutions to anticipated problems: _____

_____

_____

Shipper's normal schedule:

Date   Product/Quantity   Destination

_____   _____   _____

_____   _____   _____

Anticipated additional shipping costs due to strike:

_____

_____

Exhibit 14

ALTERNATE SHIPPER CONTACTS

Prepared by _____

Date prepared _____

Alternate shipper _____

Person contacted _____

Title _____

Telephone number _____

Address _____

Date contacted _____

Dates and equipment available:

Date	Equipment Available	Can Deliver To:
_____	_____	_____
_____	_____	_____
_____	_____	_____
_____	_____	_____

Anticipated costs in excess of normal shipping arrangements: _____

_____

_____

Exhibit 15

PRO RATA CUSTOMER DELIVERIES

Prepared by _____

Date prepared _____

Customer _____

Person contacted _____

Title _____

Telephone number _____

Date contacted _____

Normal delivery dates and quantities:

Date	Product/Quantity	Shipper
_____	_____	_____
_____	_____	_____
_____	_____	_____
_____	_____	_____

Customer will accept pro rata deliveries as follows:

Date	Product/Quantity	Shipper
_____	_____	_____
_____	_____	_____
_____	_____	_____
_____	_____	_____

Exhibit 16

POTENTIAL SUBCONTRACTOR CONTACTS

Prepared by _____

Date prepared _____

Subcontractor _____

Person contacted _____

Title _____

Date contacted _____

Contacted regarding (operation to be performed):

_____

_____

Tentative schedule:

Pick-up Date	Return Date	Unit Cost	Delivery To
_____	_____	_____	_____
_____	_____	_____	_____
_____	_____	_____	_____
_____	_____	_____	_____

Subcontract agreement to be prepared by: _____

Subsequent contact scheduled for _____

Costs in excess of normal in-plant production:

_____

_____

_____

Exhibit 17

PERSONNEL ESTIMATE - NONSTRIKING EMPLOYEES

Prepared by _____ Unit _____
                    (Foreman)

Foreman reports to _____ Date _____

1. Unit Employees

   Job Title (skill)   Number

   _____   _____

   _____   _____

   _____   _____

   _____   _____

   _____   _____

2. Estimate of Nonstrikers

   Name   Job Title

   _____   _____

   _____   _____

   _____   _____

   _____   _____

   _____   _____

   _____   _____

3. With the employees named in 2., above, this unit could
   maintain the following levels of normal production:

   a. _____% with no overtime

   b. _____% working six 8-hour days

   c. _____% working seven 8-hour days

Exhibit 17 (continued)

4. Estimated weekly overtime costs:

   3. b. $_____

   3. c. $_____

5. To maintain 100% of normal production, the following additional employees would be required:

   a. With no overtime: Skill _____ Number _____

   _____ _____

   _____ _____

   b. Six 8-hour days _____ _____

   _____ _____

   _____ _____

   c. Seven 8-hour days _____ _____

   _____ _____

6. Estimated weekly overtime costs:

   5. b. $_____

   5. c. $_____

7. Names of retirees, former employees, others, who may be available for work: _____

   _____

   _____

8. Anticipated personnel problems during strike: _____

   _____

   _____

   _____

Exhibit 18

PRODUCTION CAPABILITIES (PERSONNEL)

Prepared by
_____

Date prepared
_____

Based on foremen estimates as of _____, production could be maintained as follows:

1. With nonstriking employees only:

Unit	Total Employees	% No Overtime	% Six 8-hr. Days	% Seven 8-hr. Days
____	_____	_____	_____	_____
____	_____	_____	_____	_____
____	_____	_____	_____	_____
____	_____	_____	_____	_____
____	_____	_____	_____	_____

Estimate of weekly over-time cost: Estimate of weekly over-time cost:

$_____ $_____

2. 100% of normal production could be maintained with additional employees as follows:

	No Overtime		Six 8-hr. Days		Seven 8-hr. Days	
Unit	Skills	No.	Skills	No.	Skills	No.
____	_____	___	_____	___	_____	___
____	_____	___	_____	___	_____	___
____	_____	___	_____	___	_____	___
____	_____	___	_____	___	_____	___

Exhibit 18 (continued)

Unit	Skills	No.	Skills	No.	Skills	No.
___	_____	__	_____	__	_____	__
	_____	__	_____	__	_____	__
___	_____	__	_____	__	_____	__
	_____	__	_____	__	_____	__
___	_____	__	_____	__	_____	__
	_____	__	_____	__	_____	__
Total No.		__		__		__

Estimate of weekly over-time cost:

$_____ $_____

Exhibit 19

PRODUCTION OFFICE AND STAFF EMPLOYEES-

ALTERNATE SKILLS

Prepared by

Date prepared

Name	Dept.	Shift	Ext.	Job	Alternate Skills

Exhibit 20

ALL NON-BARGAINING UNIT EMPLOYEES-

ALTERNATE SKILLS

Prepared by

Date prepared

Name	Dept.	Shift	Ext.	Job	Alt. Skills	Reports to

Exhibit 21

PRODUCTION TRAINEES

Permanent full time jobs are now available for production trainees. Company-paid training for exciting,
skilled jobs with a growing manufacturer. Earn while
you learn. No experience required but you must have
mechanical aptitude and be willing to work long hours.
Apply at _____, 1111 Main Street, 7 AM - 7 PM. If
the personnel office is not open, ask a security officer to direct you to the second floor, Room 211.

EXPERIENCED ELECTRONIC TECHNICIANS NEEDED NOW!

Full time permanent jobs available now! Lots of overtime. If you have 2-3 years experience in _____,
come in or call today: _____, 1111 Main Street, telephone 555-5555. Out of town, call collect. Labor dispute in progress. Personnel office open 24 hours, Monday through Saturday.

STRIKE IN PROGRESS!

Full time, permanent jobs open now for assemblers, lathe
operators, welders, sheet metal mechanics and other skills.
Qualified persons can start from $____ to $____ per hour.
Pick your shift and work up to 70 hours per week. _____,
1111 Main Street, telephone (219) 555-5555. Excellent
working conditions, great benefits, secure parking, company cafeteria. An equal opportunity employer (MF)

Exhibit 22

"STAND BY" NEW EMPLOYEES

Prepared by
_____

Date prepared
_____

Name	Address & Phone	Skill	Date of Interview	Date Available	Start Rate	Training Needed
___	___	___	___	___	___	___
___	___	___	___	___	___	___
___	___	___	___	___	___	___
___	___	___	___	___	___	___
___	___	___	___	___	___	___
___	___	___	___	___	___	___
___	___	___	___	___	___	___
___	___	___	___	___	___	___
___	___	___	___	___	___	___
___	___	___	___	___	___	___

Exhibit 23

NEW AND CURRENT EMPLOYEE TRAINING REQUIREMENTS

Prepared by _____

Date prepared _____

Course	Instructor	Start/End	Place	Course Length	Class Size	Est. Cost
_____	_____	_____	_____	_____	_____	_____
_____	_____	_____	_____	_____	_____	_____
_____	_____	_____	_____	_____	_____	_____
_____	_____	_____	_____	_____	_____	_____
_____	_____	_____	_____	_____	_____	_____
_____	_____	_____	_____	_____	_____	_____
_____	_____	_____	_____	_____	_____	_____

Exhibit 24

AVAILABLE HOUSING

Prepared by
_____

Date prepared
_____

Type	Address	Mo. Cost	Lease Required?	Near Bus?	Distance From Plant
Rooms					
___	___	___	___	___	___
___	___	___	___	___	___
___	___	___	___	___	___
Apts.					
___	___	___	___	___	___
___	___	___	___	___	___
___	___	___	___	___	___
Houses					
___	___	___	___	___	___
___	___	___	___	___	___
___	___	___	___	___	___
YMCA	___	___	___	___	___
YWCA	___	___	___	___	___

Exhibit 25

ACKNOWLEDGEMENT OF RECEIPT OF CHECK

TO: _____, Inc.

    I acknowledge that I have received today check number _____, and that this check in the amount of $_____ satisfies all monies due me, including accrued vacation, through and including today's date.

                                _____
                                  Name

                                  _____
                                  Date

Exhibit 26

SCHEDULE FOR FOREMAN TRAINING

Foreman Group	1st Session Date/Time	2nd Session Date/Time	Location	Discussion Leader
_____	_____	_____	_____	_____

Foremen in Group:

_____	_____	_____
_____	_____	_____
_____	_____	_____

Exhibit 27

SECURITY CONTRACTOR CONTACT

Prepared by _____

Date prepared _____

Company _____

Person contacted _____

Title _____

Telephone number _____

Specially trained "strike force"? _____

Strikes recently worked in this area: _____

_____

How many contract guards recommended for us? _____

Strike-experienced supervisor available? _____

What equipment does the company have available (vans,

radios, etc.)? _____

How much notice is required before company's force can be

on site? _____

(Contact persons with firms the contractor has worked

strikes for and also the police in those cities.)

Other considerations: _____

_____

Exhibit 28

COMPANY SECURITY FORCE - MAXIMUM WORK SCHEDULE

Employee	Normal Schedule		Shift	Hours
	S___M___T___W___TH___F___S___		_____	_____
_____	Revised Schedule		Shift	Hours
	S___M___T___W___TH___F___S___		_____	_____

(Example)

Employee	Normal Schedule		Shift	Hours
	S_x_M_x_T_x_W_x_TH_x_F___S___		2nd	8/40
M. Dillon	Revised Schedule		Shift	Hours
	S_x_M_x_T_x_W_x_TH_x_F_x_S___		2nd	12/72

(Estimate of weekly overtime cost (total company security force): $_____)

(Scheduling revisions will depend on the size of your own security force and the number of contract guards brought in. In any event, it is a good idea to have as many of your own people as feasible on duty at any given time. If the contract guards prove overzealous, your employees can provide a calming influence.)

Exhibit 29

OUTSIDE AGENCY CONTACT

Prepared by _____

Date prepared _____

Agency _____

Person(s) contacted _____

Title(s) _____

Date of meeting _____

Length of meeting _____

Matters discussed _____

_____

_____

Summary of discussion _____

_____

_____

Additional meetings scheduled or anticipated? _____

_____

Were results of meeting satisfactory? _____

If not, why, and steps to be taken to correct deficiencies:

_____

_____

Exhibit 30

DAILY GUARD FORCE STATIONS

Prepared by _____

Date prepared _____

(Completed here as an example)

Day __Monday 8-19_____ Shift __2nd_____

Post Location	Company Security	Contract Guards
Front entrance	1	2
Atop main office	0	1
Atop warehouse B	0	1
Parking lot	2	0
Side entrance	1	2
Rear entrance	1	2
Main guard station	1	3
Production area	2	1
Plant front door	1	1
Plant rear door	1	1
Inside warehouse A	0	1
Inside warehouse B	0	1
Total	10	16

(Prepare chart for each day and shift)

Exhibit 31

INCIDENT REPORT

Nature of incident _____

_____

_____

Date, time, and exact location of incident _____

_____

Names or descriptions of all persons involved _____

_____

_____

Names or descriptions of witnesses _____

_____

_____

Describe the incident in detail - who did and said what to whom, what objects (rocks, cars, nails, etc.) were involved, how the incident started and how it ended, etc.

_____

_____

_____

Report prepared by _____

Address and telephone _____

Employed by _____

Today's date _____

Exhibit 32

FACILITY DAILY INSPECTION SCHEDULE

Prepared by _____

Date prepared _____

Day _____

Parking lot	_____AM	_____AM	_____PM	_____PM
Warehouse A	_____AM	_____AM	_____PM	_____PM
Warehouse B	_____AM	_____AM	_____PM	_____PM
Production	_____AM	_____AM	_____PM	_____PM
Main office bldg.	_____AM	_____AM	_____PM	_____PM
Transformer room	_____AM	_____AM	_____PM	_____PM
Perimeter fencing	_____AM	_____AM	_____PM	_____PM

(Note: Assign two security people to make each inspection together.)

Exhibit 33

ALTERNATE SOURCES FOR ESSENTIAL SERVICES

Prepared by _____

Date prepared _____

(Completed here as an example.)

Service: _____ Electricity _____

Company contacted: _____ R & H Electric - 1616 Elm _____

Person contacted: _____ Clyde Hubbell _____

Title: _____ General manager _____

Telephone: _____ 555-5554 _____

Date contacted: _____ 8-22 _____

Assistance available: _____ portable generators _____

Equipment available: _____ has 4 on hand, can get 3 more by

_____ 9-1; he delivers and sets up _____

Cost: _____ $60 per day each; includes _____

_____ delivery and set up _____

Anticipated problems: _____ none; employees are not union ___

Exhibit 34

RENTAL AGENCY CONTACT

Prepared by _____

Date prepared _____

Agency _____

Person contacted _____

Title _____ Telephone _____ Date ____

Rents:	Yes/No	Quantity Available	Delivers?	Cost/Day/Unit
cots	_____	_____	_____	_____
sheets	_____	_____	_____	_____
blankets	_____	_____	_____	_____
pillows	_____	_____	_____	_____
tables	_____	_____	_____	_____
chairs	_____	_____	_____	_____
stoves	_____	_____	_____	_____
silverware	_____	_____	_____	_____
TVs	_____	_____	_____	_____
radios	_____	_____	_____	_____
game tables	_____	_____	_____	_____
dishwasher	_____	_____	_____	_____
washing machine	_____	_____	_____	_____
clothes dryer	_____	_____	_____	_____
_____	_____	_____	_____	_____

Exhibit 35

FOOD CATERER CONTACT

<u>Prepared by</u>

<u>Date prepared</u>

Company _____

Person contacted _____

Title _____

Telephone number _____

Date contacted _____

In-plant facilities required for service: _____

_____

_____

Can provide _____ meals per day for _____ employees

Provides round-the-clock service? _____

Cost: _____

_____

Sample menu:

Breakfast   Lunch   Dinner   Snacks

_____   _____   _____   _____

_____   _____   _____   _____

_____   _____   _____   _____

_____   _____   _____   _____

Exhibit 36

INVENTORY OF NON-PRODUCTION MATERIAL

Prepared by _____

Date prepared _____

(Completed here as examples)

Material _____ liquid shop soap _____

Normal daily usage _____ 2 gallons _____

On hand this date _____ 9 gallons _____

Anticipated supply/delivery problems ___ none _____

_____

Recommendation _____ order as needed; keep

_____ 28 gallons on hand ___

Material _____ shop towels _____

Normal daily usage _____ 200 - 225 _____

On hand this date _____ about 1000 _____

Anticipated supply/delivery problems ___ supply company __

employees are union, so is truck driver _____

Recommendation _____ purchase 1500 towels;

_____ launder in-plant _____

Exhibit 37

DAILY LOG - STRIKE CONTROL CENTER

Day/Date _____ (12:01 AM - 12:00 PM)

1. Picket   Time: Number/Names/Descriptions Sign Wording
   Location   From/To

   _____ _____ _____ _____

   _____ _____ _____ _____

   _____ _____ _____ _____

   _____ _____ _____ _____

2. Incidents Involving Pickets

   a. _____ (report attached)

   b. _____ (report attached)

   c. _____ (report attached)

3. Handbills Distributed

   Time   Location

   _____ _____ (sample attached)

   _____ _____ (sample attached)

4. Carriers Refusing To Cross Picket Line

   Company   Time/Location   Company notified

   _____ _____ _____

   _____ _____ _____

   _____ _____ _____

5. Calls To Local Police

   Time   Reason

   _____ _____ (report attached)

   _____ _____ (report attached)

Exhibit 37 (continued)

6. New Hires

Name	Job	Dept./Shift	Start Date
_____	_____	_____	_____
_____	_____	_____	_____
_____	_____	_____	_____
_____	_____	_____	_____
_____	_____	_____	_____

7. Contacts With Foremen

Foreman	Dept./Shift	Comments	Action Required
_____	_____	_____	_____
_____	_____	_____	_____
_____	_____	_____	_____
_____	_____	_____	_____
_____	_____	_____	_____

8. Contract Negotiations

   Scheduled? _____ (copy of minutes attached)

9. EOC Meeting

   Scheduled? _____ (copy of minutes attached)

10. Other Committee Meetings

   Production? _____ (copy of minutes attached)

   Production Support? _____ (copy of minutes attached)

   Strike Control? _____ (copy of minutes attached)

11. Production Report (attached)

12. Supplier Problems

Exhibit 37 (continued)

Supplier	Problem	Action Taken
_____	_____	_____
_____	_____	_____
_____	_____	_____

13. Customer Problems

Customer	Problem	Action Taken
_____	_____	_____
_____	_____	_____
_____	_____	_____

14. Material Problems

Material	Problem	Action Taken
_____	_____	_____
_____	_____	_____
_____	_____	_____

15. Employees Transferred

Name	From/To	Probable Duration
_____	_____	_____
_____	_____	_____
_____	_____	_____

16. Strikers Requesting Reinstatement

Name	Circumstances	Action Taken
_____	_____	_____
_____	_____	_____
_____	_____	_____

Exhibit 37 (continued)

17. Other Contacts From Strikers (Describe)

_____

_____

_____

_____

18. Contacts With Union Officials (Describe)

_____

_____

_____

19. New Rumors Circulating (Describe each and action taken)

_____

_____

_____

20. Estimate of Strike Cost

    To Company: Today $_____   To Date $_____

    To Strikers: Today $_____   To Date $_____

21. Inquiries Received

    From   Question   Answer Given

    _____   _____   _____

    _____   _____   _____

    _____   _____   _____

    _____   _____   _____

Exhibit 38

CUMULATIVE STRIKE COSTS

Prepared by _____

Date prepared _____

Day/Date _____

Item	Cost Today	Cost To Date
Overtime	_____	_____
Legal fees	_____	_____
Shipping	_____	_____
Security	_____	_____
Training	_____	_____
Warehousing	_____	_____
Subcontracting	_____	_____
Recruiting	_____	_____
Facility Improvements	_____	_____
_____	_____	_____
_____	_____	_____
_____	_____	_____
_____	_____	_____
_____	_____	_____
_____	_____	_____
_____	_____	_____

Exhibit 39

PRESS RELEASE

A strike by the _____ union, local # _____, was instituted at 6:00 AM today against _____. The company regrets this action by the union and considers it unjustified
by any reasonable standard.

The company intends to continue operations without
interruption and without reduction of either the quantity
or quality of our fine products. The company has resolved
to fully meet its obligations to its customers, the community it serves, and its employees.

The union struck after twenty-six lengthy bargaining sessions. The issues had been narrowed from over
thirty to less than five. The economic package offered
by the company would have placed the striking employees'
already competitive wage among the highest in the city
for the work performed. In the interest of maintaining
the lowest reasonable production costs, the company could
not in good conscious offer more.

Again, _____ intends that normal operations will
continue. To the extent this walkout causes temporary in-
convenience, we ask your indulgence.

The company feels this action by the union is detri-
mental to the best interests of all concerned. We feel
the union leadership has acted in haste and without seri-

Exhibit 39 (continued)

---

ously considering the effect this strike could have on the employees it represents and the community in which we live. For our part we accept this challenge to sound fiscal management and will meet it responsibly and with resolve.

Your support and understanding during this unfortunate incident will be greatly appreciated.

Exhibit 40

INFORMATION FOR NEW EMPLOYEES

Welcome to _____. We are very pleased to have you as a new member of our family.

You are scheduled to begin work on _____, _____ at _____ AM/PM. Your regular workweek is _____, _____, _____, _____, and _____. Each shift is _____ hours. Lunch time on your shift is from _____ to _____. You will have two coffee breaks each shift of 20 minutes duration. Your foreman's name is _____.

Come to the personnel office a few minutes before the start of your first shift and you will be accompanied to your unit and introduced to your foreman.

You have been given a parking sticker. It should be attached to the left side (from the driver's viewpoint) of your bumper before you report to work.

If you need information concerning apartments or other housing, call this office, extension _____, or come by.

As you know, a strike against the company is in progress. All reasonable measures have been taken to insure your safety, and there is no need for concern.

If you are approached by pickets or for any other reason feel threatened, please contact Security at extension _____, any time day or night.

Exhibit 40 (continued)

You are scheduled to attend an employee benefits orientation on _____, _____, at _____ AM/PM. Your foreman knows of this and will give you directions to the room in which the session will be held.

If you are scheduled for training, your foreman will tell you the time and place you are to report.

Again, welcome to our company.

Exhibit 41

(LETTER TO STRIKING EMPLOYEES)

Dear Mr. _____:

It has been a week now since the union called a strike against our company, and during that time I have thought long and hard about the events leading up to it.

As I see it, it is simply a case of a union making unreasonable demands on our company. I don't know how the union justified the demands it is making on the company to the employees it represents, but I want you to know it would not be in the best interest of any of us for the company to give in to them.

I honestly feel the 7 per cent general increase the company has offered is very reasonable and should have been accepted.

Aside from business considerations I regret this strike for other reasons. I know many of you personally, and I know being out of work can be difficult.

I am writing you today to tell you that if you would like to come back to work you are welcome. Your job is waiting. The decision is yours, and I sincerely hope what you decide is best for you and your family.

It is only fair to add that the company must also do what it feels is best, and in that regard it has been decided to begin hiring permanent replacements two weeks from

Exhibit 41 (continued)

---

today. I tell you this not to try to frighten you into
returning, but because I want you to have all the facts.
Therefore, I cannot tell you your job will be open in-
definitely.

   If it is your decision to return, please contact Mr.
_____ in personnel, telephone number 555-5555 or come
by.

                    Yours sincerely,

                    _____

Exhibit 42

(INFORMATION FLYER TO EMPLOYEES)

TO: ALL EMPLOYEES

As you probably already know, _____ union has today called a strike against our company. The company has for several months been trying to negotiate a new contract with this union to replace the contract which recently expired. However, we have not been able to resolve all the union's demands, and the union has seen fit to call this strike.

The company regrets that the union has taken this action, and the company continues to believe that the position it has taken in these negotiations is in the best interest of all employees.

It is the company's firm resolve to continue normal operations.

During the strike you will no doubt see persons represented by the union 'picketing' the plant entrances. Please be advised that these persons have no legal right to interfere in any manner with your entering or leaving the plant. They have no right to ask your name or to obtain any information whatsoever from you. If any of these persons attempts to hinder your entrance to or exit from the plant, or makes insulting comments to you, or by word or action threatens your safety, please report the incident to Security at once.

Exhibit 42 (continued)

Again, the company intends to continue operations in as near normal fashion as possible. There is no feeling among management that the strike will affect the workload of the company, so do not be alarmed for your job.

To the extent that there are temporarily some work schedule or other changes from the normal routine, please bear with us.

Your continued cooperation and support, now and in the days ahead, will be greatly appreciated.

Sincerely,

‾‾‾‾‾‾‾‾‾‾‾‾‾
(CEO)

Exhibit 43

PRODUCTION - TASK ASSIGNMENTS AND COMPLETIONS

Prepared by
_____

Date prepared
_____

Task	Assigned To	Target Date	Completion Date
1. Vendor notification	_____	_____	_____
(attach completed forms)			
2. Investigation of offsite delivery points	_____	_____	_____
(attach completed forms)			
3. Investigation of material stockpiling	_____	_____	_____
(attach completed forms)			
4. Prepare Material Status Summary	_____	_____	_____
(attach completed form)			
5. Prepare Accelerated Maintenance Schedule	_____	_____	_____
(attach completed form)			
6. Investigate storage of vulnerable equipment	_____	_____	_____
(attach completed form)			
7. Assign work order screening and investigation of machinery breakdowns	_____	_____	_____
8. Advise foremen of tool, equipment, and safety responsibilities	_____	_____	_____

Exhibit 43 (continued)

Task	Assigned To	Target Date	Completion Date
9. Pre-strike customer contacts	_____	_____	_____
(attach completed forms)			
10. Shipper contacts	_____	_____	_____
(attach completed forms)			
11. Alternate shipper contacts	_____	_____	_____
(attach completed forms)			
12. Pro-rata shipments	_____	_____	_____
(attach completed forms)			
13. Subcontractor contacts	_____	_____	_____
(attach completed forms)			
14. Foreman personnel estimates	_____	_____	_____
(attach completed forms)			
15. Overall production capability estimate	_____	_____	_____
(attach completed form)			
16. Production office and staff- alternate skills	_____	_____	_____
(attach completed form)			
17. Office employees who can be released- (Production Support Committee)	_____	_____	_____
18. Overtime requirements- transferred employees	_____	_____	_____

Exhibit 44

PRODUCTION SUPPORT - TASK ASSIGNMENTS AND COMPLETIONS

Prepared by _____

Date prepared _____

Task	Assigned To	Target Date	Completion Date
1. Alternate skills - non-bargaining unit employees	_____	_____	_____
(attach completed form)			
2. Prepare striker replacement ads; check state law regulating hiring	_____	_____	_____
(attach ads; summary of state law)			
3. Contact applicant referral sources	_____	_____	_____
(attach list)			
4. 'Stand-by' new hires	_____	_____	_____
(attach completed form)			
5. New and current employee training; coordinate with Production Committee	_____	_____	_____
(attach completed form)			
6. Investigate extended personnel office hours	_____	_____	_____
(attach report)			
7. Study of available housing	_____	_____	_____
(attach completed form)			

Exhibit 44 (continued)

Task	Assigned To	Target Date	Completion Date
8. Obtain supply of maps, bus schedules; parking locations	_____	_____	_____
9. Prepare paycheck receipt	_____	_____	_____
10. Discontinuance of fringe benefit payments	_____	_____	_____
11. Contact employment commission; names of strikers	_____	_____	_____
12. Stockpile medical supplies; attach list	_____	_____	_____
13. Contact ambulance services; attach report	_____	_____	_____
14. Arrange to employ temporary nurses	_____	_____	_____
15. Schedule foreman training	_____	_____	_____
(attach completed form)			
16. Prepare Fact Sheet- union strike history and related matters; attach	_____	_____	_____
17. Arrange for review of discipline; attach report	_____	_____	_____
18. Consult counsel re grievance handling; attach report	_____	_____	_____
19. ID badge arrangements; attach report	_____	_____	_____
20. Revised Security work schedules	_____	_____	_____
(attach completed forms)			

Exhibit 44 (continued)

Task	Assigned To	Target Date	Completion Date
21. Security contractor contacts	_____	_____	_____
(attach completed forms)			
22. Agency contacts: city police, county sheriff, FBI, state attorney general, railroad police	_____	_____	_____
(attach completed forms)			
23. Devise plan to protect employee homes; attach report	_____	_____	_____
24. Devise plan for escort of employee cars; attach report	_____	_____	_____
25. Arrange for rental of two-way radios; attach report	_____	_____	_____
26. Prepare plant maps for security guards; attach	_____	_____	_____
27. Prepare plan for package inspection; attach report	_____	_____	_____
28. Recommend additional lighting and fencing if needed; attach report	_____	_____	_____
29. Develop plan for location of guard force	_____	_____	_____
(attach completed form)			
30. Supply of binoculars, tape recorders, cameras; attach list	_____	_____	_____
31. Develop plan for testing picket line; attach	_____	_____	_____

Exhibit 44 (continued)

Task	Assigned To	Target Date	Completion Date
32. Inspect fire protection equipment; attach report	_____	_____	_____
33. Investigate riot training for security force; attach report	_____	_____	_____
34. Prepare facility security inspection schedule	_____	_____	_____
(attach completed form)			
35. Develop procedure for escort of strikers entering building; attach report	_____	_____	_____
36. Meet with utility officials	_____	_____	_____
(attach completed forms)			
37. Investigate alternate utility sources	_____	_____	_____
(attach completed forms)			
38. Meet with city regarding trash removal; attach report	_____	_____	_____
39. Prepare for employees to eat and sleep in plant; attach report	_____	_____	_____
(attach completed forms)			
40. Develop 24-hour switchboard operation; attach report	_____	_____	_____
41. Inventory non-production supplies	_____	_____	_____
(attach completed forms)			

Exhibit 45

STRIKE CONTROL - TASK ASSIGNMENTS AND COMPLETIONS

Prepared by
_____

Date prepared
_____

Task	Assigned To	Target Date	Completion Date
1. Secure and equip Strike Control Center; attach report			
2. Develop Daily Log format; attach			
3. Prepare strike cost estimate format; attach			
4. Prepare press releases; attach			
5. Plan for daily contact with departments; attach report			
6. Develop plan for picket line observation; attach			
7. Plan for record deplication; attach report			
8. Plan for 'outside' contacts; attach report			
9. New employee processing; attach report			
10. New employee welcome; attach			
11. Letter to strikers; attach			
12. Employee flyer; attach			

Index